MANY TRAILS

MANY
TRAILS

by

R. D. Symons

LONGMANS CANADA LIMITED

PRINTED AND BOUND IN CANADA

*TO THE MEMORY OF MY FATHER WHO
EQUIPPED ME FOR THE TRAIL OF LIFE*

TO THE READER

THIS BOOK is the fulfilment of a promise. Long ago, in London, a small boy sat near the hunter Selous, who had but lately returned from his African game trails. The hunter had been talking with the grown-ups — talking of buffaloes and elephants and great dark-maned lions; and in his mind the boy too peered over kopjes at great herds of game, felt the dry veldt grass beneath his feet and the clutch of thorny branches on his clothes.

To the hunter he offered his crude drawings—done in a corner of his father's studio—of the scenes he had heard of on previous visits: thick-necked eland at a water-hole, a rhinoceros charging a safari, lions lying in wait. And the hunter said, "I see that you are observant and that you like animals, and it seems you can use a pencil too. So when you are big I want you to go to Africa—or somewhere else if you like, it doesn't matter—and draw the birds and animals you will see, and write about them too, so that other people can see them and know them as well as you. Don't forget." And the boy promised. Years passed and he still remembered.

But Africa, with its snarling big cats and herds of antelope, was not for him. At sixteen he came to the Canadian prairies.

England (which meant Sussex to him)—the smooth-shouldered downs, the shingle beaches, the trim cottages by the lanes — seemed very far away.

Far away, too, seemed those days of a few months since when he had decided that Canada called him. The days when he had got up each morning to go down to the stables at Parsonage Farm for his lessons in milking under the eye of old Butchers the cowman — for he had been determined that he would not be entirely green in the land to which he was going.

Now a new life was opening up to him, and he was learning to handle horses and do chores around a ranch-yard.

And he was thrilled by it, by everything. The first night in a prairie ranch-house after the long journey across the plains. The never-to-be-forgotten feel and smell of flannelette sheets inviting to sleep, . . . with none of the preliminary warming up required of English linen. The drifting off to sleep with the tinkling of cowbells clear and insistent above the swelling frog chorus. The peremptory call in the early morning, and the sleepy stumbling out to the stables in air made keen as wine by the spring breeze.

And the birds! He couldn't name them at first, and no help was available from the boss, beyond telling a crow from a prairie chicken. But he knew his English birds — wrens are much the same the world over; pink-sided juncos are so like chaffinches that it was easy to know they were of the same family, the Fringillidae; and the feathered legs of prairie chicken showed them to be grouse. So he could roughly classify those he saw as he lay on the prairie knolls to observe them, taking time from driving the cows in at dawn, or as he tramped the oozy edges of the sloughs on Sunday afternoons. Even during week-days he sometimes left the plow at the furrow's end while he penetrated a wolf-willow thicket or explored a rock pile in the quest that led him on.

And always he sketched.

Then, while reading the *No' West Farmer* (a magazine now, alas, defunct), he found a short article on prairie birds by Dr. Speechly of Pilot Mound, Manitoba, and to him he sent some of his coloured drawings with a request for information. His birds were named for him and the questions answered. He never met the Doctor — which is a regret — but he has never forgotten the kindness and the encouragement. If Dr. Speechly is still living when this is in print, he will remember, and know the gratitude that is felt.

Soon the boy had served his apprenticeship of sawer of wood, milker of cows, and plower of garden patches; he was able to handle a horse well enough to help on the range and follow the cattle trails.

Still he pursued his quest as pipits rose from the grass before his pony's hoofs.

Then the war of 1914. But even during those grey days he heard the skylark singing above the torn Somme and saw brown hares in the beet fields. Stumbling with his platoon through the debris-choked streets of La Forête, he heard a little brown wren singing above the whine and crash of shells, and looking up, saw it perched on a block of crumbling masonry.

Then back to Canada, but this time to the mountain province of British Columbia, where he learned the diamond hitch on the Chilcotin pack trails.

But the prairies beckoned again, and next he was homesteading in central Saskatchewan. Then his all-absorbing love for birds and animals led to a position as game and fishery officer, a position which at one station brought him much among the Cree Indians of the Saskatchewan River, for whom he learned to have a great liking.

Finally transferred to the crisp North with its endless forests and maze of waterways and lakes, he travelled the gleaming canoe routes by summer, by winter the drifted and tortuous toboggan trails.

So he asks to take you in this book from the dry plains, where the dust-devils skip across the border, to the wooded hills and flowery prairies of mid-Saskatchewan; from the snowy peaks of the Cascades to the cold muskegs of northern Manitoba. He will try to show you something of the life of fur and feather and hoof and fin which he has seen.

But if he has digressed from the underlying theme and written of people too, it is because in this workaday world few of us are able to desert our fellows for the study of nature alone, as did Thoreau once. Those of whom he has written are those with whom he has worked; and the natural result of rubbing shoulders with all sorts of people is to appreciate them.

The stories of the French-Canadian rancher, Henry Clay Johnston, and Ma Parsons show some of the diversity of the cultural threads which are being woven into the fabric of the Canadian nation. The stories are as true as he can write them — that is, the only falsifications are such as are necessary to conceal real names and real places; but in no way is essential truth tampered with.

So if you can feel the soft chinook on your cheeks, hear the laugh of water mingled with the cries of night-birds, or catch a glimpse of the bull moose feeding in the alder thickets, then a promise will have been kept.

ACKNOWLEDGEMENTS

The author acknowledges with thanks the courtesy of the editors of the *Family Herald* for permission to reprint the story of the buffalo hunt, which first appeared in that magazine. His thanks are due also to the editor of *Canadian Cattlemen* in connection with the story of Eagle Lake Henry's black horse.

CONTENTS

GLOSSARY

ā-koosā (Cree)

It is well.

bench

A plateau.

bluff

A small grove of poplar and willow trees on the prairie.

brulé (French)

Burnt-over land, often with a lot of criss-cross logs scattered about. In travelling, one avoids it as much as possible.

buzzard

Any hawks of the genus Buteo. As used here, commonly means the ferrugineous rough-legged hawk.

cavvy

Spare horses for use during round-up (Spanish *cabello*).

chickamun (Chinook)

Money.

concession

A government grant of land. In Ontario, the First Concession consisted of the parcels of land on either side of the main roads. As these were settled, a Second Concession would be opened up, then a Third, and so on.

cooney

A tarpaulin tied under a chuck-wagon box as a receptacle for dry wood or other fuel.

cultus (Chinook)

Bad.

cultus coulee

(Literally, "bad running.") Bad travel — that is, aimless wandering.

democrat

An American word meaning a light spring wagon.

draw	A shallow valley, of no great size and without a stream. Low, narrow flat area between rolling hills.
Haver	Cowboy way of saying Havre, a cow town in Montana.
haze	To gather and drive stock.
helo (Chinook)	No, nothing. "He helo hat stop" — he has no hat (on).
hyu (Chinook)	Much, many, very.
Irvine pale beds	Pale outcroppings of the Cretaceous period occurring commonly throughout the semi-arid parts of the great plains.
Keesa-, Kisa-, or Kitche-Manitoo	The Great Spirit of the Indian religion.
keewadin (Cree)	The north-west wind (which brings the blizzard).
klootch (Chinook)	Wife or woman.
loper	The grey wolf of the plains, a subspecific form of the wolf family common to both hemispheres; also known as the buffalo wolf. The Spanish name is *lobo,* and this word was brought from the South by the Texas cattlemen who came north with their cattle. It has been corrupted to "loper" and "loafer."
Mishi Mokoman-uk (Cree)	United States cavalry. (Literally "the long knives," *i.e.* cavalry sabres.)

moostoos (Cree)	Buffalo.
mossy-horn steer	As a steer gets older the base of the horns becomes corrugated and scabby. Hence, a steer five or six years old.
mowitch (Chinook)	Deer.
Nihi-o-wuk (Cree)	The Indian nations.
pasture	In general, applied to a grazing area smaller than a range, enclosed by a fence and not far from the ranch buildings.
prairie wool	Heavy growth of prairie grass which becomes curled and dimpled, and when mowed cleaves together in the swath like wool from a sheep's back. Composed of a number of different grasses and herbs, of which rough fescue is the most prominent.
range	A large grazing area, formerly unfenced ("open range") but now often enclosed by a fence.
Red Fife wheat	A famous grain grown in Manitoba years ago. Unknown now.
rustle	To obtain with some effort. As applied to grazing cattle, it means to get at grass that is buried under snow. To say that a man is "a good rustler" means that he is active and a good provider.
sand-hills	1. The great sand-hills of Saskatchewan. 2. The Indian hereafter or heaven.

sic tum-tum (Chinook)	Sad thoughts.
sinkhole	A small depression in the prairie, usually with alkaline springs below it and therefore having no herbage. Its condition varies with the water level and is very unpredictable. One day it may be dry and hard, and another day a real trap for stock, which find themselves enmired.
skookum (Siwash)	Strong.
slough	In Western Canada, a pond rather than a bog.
soniow okimow (Cree)	Indian agent.
"Stag" breaking ploughs	So called because made by the John Deere Company.
strong woods	The great northern forests.
stump rancher	A rancher who operates in semi-timbered country. After he has built his log house and corrals, there are stumps left about. Sometimes, in derision, it is applied to small settlers who "grow nothing but stumps." I think I came under the first category to my friends and the latter to my enemies.
turkey	A cowboy's bedroll.
weetigo (Cree)	A bad spirit.

windflower

The prairie anemone, found all over the great plains. It is commonly called by this name in the cattle country, and crocus on the more eastern prairie. It is also called the Pasque flower because it usually blooms about Easter time. It is about the first blossom on the prairie in the spring.

wrangle field

A fenced field in which saddle horses are turned loose when not in use.

START OF THE TRAIL

CHAPTER ONE

My Father

MY FATHER was a man of very definite ideas. A true Victorian by birth and upbringing, he was yet a heretic in those days of orthodoxy. An artist himself, he followed Whistler into the no man's land of those who differed from the hidebound opinions of the Royal Academy Board. Always a poor man, he astounded his acquaintances by referring to himself as the richest man in England.

Just as today we bow with respect to our standard of living, so in my childhood the national household god was respectability—a god to whom, however, my bearded male parent refused to make obeisance. Example: respectability in the late nineties had already drawn up a family blueprint of not more than three children—preferably two boys and a girl. My father had nine; I was the eighth, and the seventh son. Father would have been as happy with nineteen, and he and my mother between them handled the nine more easily than any modern couple manage one.

Of course, no one had heard of child psychology in those days. Frustration was an unknown word. Self-expression was a matter to be approached only by artists, poets, and musicians, and then only after they had passed through the hard but necessary schooling whereby they acquired a skeleton upon which to drape the "expressive" flesh.

For us youngsters it was early rising, bread-and-milk nursery breakfast, pothooks and multiplication tables in the schoolroom (the same day nursery, so called, when not used for games or meals), brisk walks, and eat just exactly what was put before you—or go without. In a thoroughly disciplined and efficiently managed household, why should it not have been easy for our parents to raise us?

Mother and Father did not have to go into a huddle and worry about why Molly was slow in her arithmetic on Tuesdays, or why Stephen looked with disgust at his perfectly good rice pudding on Saturday. It never occurred to them that the slightest word of correction might mysteriously "hurt" Molly for life; or that Stephen was perhaps "allergic" to rice, and forcing him to eat it might give him a "complex." (Goodness—reading back, I dimly realize how many new words we have cumbered ourselves with since 1914.)

What my father did know was that Molly's arithmetic always improved after he tore her paper across and wrote "Rotten—feeble—do it again." Likewise, he usually did *not* need to step into the nursery and roar (yes, he roared—like all proper fathers, be they human or animal) for Stephen to wolf his pudding. As often as not, Father's step in the passage was quite enough, thank you.

He hated cats. Of course, it is a very "bad influence" on susceptible little children for their fathers to hate anything, let alone demonstrate that hatred. But if our old cat, or some of her numerous progeny, happened to invade his studio, down would go his palette and brush, and seizing one of the numerous swords that were always to hand, he would chase that cat down the stairs, slashing away and shouting for dear life—but the target was always missed, of course. I am afraid I cannot say as much for the banisters; we children used to count the notches on them.

Those swords I must explain a bit, because perhaps my women readers might imagine they were kept chiefly for this, and for other disciplinary purposes too horrible to hint at. In point of fact the collection of Indian tulwars, cavalry sabres, Turkish scimitars, and a host of others, were simply artist's props. They were very useful during those periods of financial stress when Father had to illustrate stories in the *Strand* and *Wide World* "to keep the pot boiling," as he used to say. He hated it, but did the work with the greatest enthusiasm.

We children often had to sit for him (and later for our elder brother) at a penny per hour, with a rest every fifteen minutes. Splendid training in sitting still. Pocket money, other than the above salary, was a penny a week to age fourteen, and then tuppence. Church was very compulsory, and likewise family prayers.

Well, you have seen something of the picture—and now do you wonder that we absolutely adored our father? What other children

4

had such a father?—a father who painted jolly pictures, and actually paid you for sitting all dressed up like a Turk, an Indian Chief, or a Zulu—-and as if that were not enough reward, also told you the story he was illustrating, in short, vivid sentences fairly dripping with healthy gore. A father who roared like a lion one minute and chuckled like a Cheshire cat the next, who chased Old Nokomis (the cat, of course, and you can guess why the name) with swords; who never gave the slightest leeway when it came to matters of obedience, who smoked a strong pipe, and who tickled you with his beard when he kissed you good night.

You will also have gathered that this love and adoration was based on a very firm foundation of respect. Father was a *father,* not a pal. He never tried to be a pal—thank God.

This is about my father; but since he and my mother were inseparable, I must mention her too. She was twenty years younger than Father, but had it been necessary she would have been quite capable of holding her own. It was not necessary.

Mother was a gold medallist of the Royal Academy of Music and played divinely. She also composed. After we, one by one, attained the ripe age of ten, we were required to be in the drawing-room for one hour after dinner. (I mean Father's and Mother's dinner—we had tea in the nursery much earlier.) During that hour we sat in our separate chairs and did not move—although I expect we did some wriggling about when we felt ticklish. And Mother played Beethoven, Chopin, Liszt, Franck, Schubert, Mendelssohn, and Grieg. (I especially love Grieg.) She composed a special little "Baby Song" for each of her children while they were still babies. I can sing them all yet.

We did not know we were being educated, we just drew in music with our mother's playing. We did not know we were being trained in good manners. We just knew we had to sit still and not interrupt the music by talking. We loved those evenings, and thanks to them I love music and know how to listen to it now.

Family prayers followed. We did not know we were being taught religion, we just knew about God in a perfectly natural manner. Then, back to the nursery and bed, after which Mother read from the current book. When very small, of course, we had *Just So Stories* or *Alice in Wonderland,* or tales by Hans Christian Andersen. (I still read *The Snow Queen.*) Thirty years later, I found I could tell all the *Just So Stories* to my children by heart in almost the exact original wording.

When we grew older, it was Scott, Dickens, Stevenson, and Cooper. In this way we had gone through *The Antiquary, The Last Days of Pompeii, David Copperfield, Treasure Island, The Last of the Mohicans,* and *Handy Andy* (how we roared—my mother was a dramatic reader) by the time I was twelve. But *we* did not know we were being educated in good literature.

Of course, I had been reading myself since I was six or seven; but those were mostly books on natural history and travel, with of course old friends like Henty and Ballantyne. I was just getting into my stride with Kipling and David Livingstone. The reason I can pick up a "dry" book of Scott's (no illustrations, and small print for hundreds of pages) and enjoy it today is that this volume is known to me as a tried and true childhood friend.

At seven, we were supposed to have come to the age of reason. It was a great event, and heavy duties were laid upon the initiate. Perhaps the most important one was to write or illustrate, once monthly, in our family journal, *The Hornbeam Magazine*. This had been started about 1895 by my eldest brother, known by the time I was seven (1905) as the "Hairy Beardster" by reason of his addiction to the razor. The magazine was a monthly one, given to Father and Mother on the third of each month. In mid-December the twelve issues were retrieved from Mother's room and bound as an annual in gay red and black, with a brand-new coloured frontispiece. Thereafter, it took end place in the snug row of its older brothers on a shelf by Mother's bed.

The frontispiece was by Mark Lancelot, later an artist; the editor was Philip, later a Benedictine monk, and of course he handled the leading articles as well as musical and ecclesiastical subjects. Bookbinder and "printer" (the "printing" was actually pen-and-ink writing in a copperplate hand) was William Christian Jr., now of New York, who was also an authority on mechanics and reviewed all new internal-combustion equipages. Sister Molly—later Sister Mary Agnese—did recipes, holiday poems and watering-places. Authority on angling, bicycling, and kindred subjects was Stephen White, later an engineer. A rather smudgy artist, I fear—probably too much rice pudding. Stephen got his wings in the old R.F.C. and his Sopwith Camel was shot down in 1917.

Specialist in mammalogy and painting was James Anthony, R.A. student, who was killed in action in 1916.

John Martyn, later a gunnery officer, explained all military matters and wrote splendid articles on the Russian-Japanese war then in progress. According to his theory, the Japanese should have licked the "Roosians" six months before they did.

I myself, now a stump rancher in the Peace River Country, contributed bird lore with extensive and colourful drawings, also essays on how to grow turnips and the points of Wyandotte poultry.

The youngest of all, Elizabeth Ann, contributed rather sentimental verse and fashion drawings. She did professional fashion drawings later till she married her soldier.

There you have the nine of us. As we used to sing it, "a rare old, fair old, rickety-rackety crew."

Besides the *Hornbeam* (named for our house, the Hornbeams at Robertsbridge), we had a great many duties. As Christmas approached we gathered tons of holly leaves and berries and under Molly's supervision we threaded them into great boas to criss-cross the dining-room ceiling. Night after night we pricked our hands to the steady reading of *Barnaby Rudge* or *Bracebridge Hall*. From seven on, nursery days behind us, each member of the family made his or her bed, and there was no getting out of the chore. We had an upstairs maid, but I venture to say we gave her less work and more respect (even though she had to call us Master this or Miss that) than many young people now give their mothers.

In the spring and summer we took care of a really large garden. At ten I got my first poultry, Wyandottes, and thereafter my spare time was divided between caring for them (at a profit, too; Mother gave me ninepence a dozen for eggs, and I bought my own feed) and walking the fields with shepherds or the woods with the game-keeper. Later I had canaries, and still later budgerigars. Incidentally, I made enough from these hobbies to pretty well outfit me to come to Canada when I was sixteen.

Naturally, we all painted more or less. I was allowed a corner in Father's studio to paint my birds in. Father did not know an awful lot about birds, but he knew drawing, and if mine did not pass muster he wasted no time in polite comment, nor did he (as we are told we must do now) try to find something encouraging to say. Oh no! "What kind of mess is this?" he would thunder and trample the offensive thing under foot just like one of Kipling's elephants. "Use your eye—and your pencil, man," he would add, "like this." At that, he would grind his thumb in whatever paint happened to be on his palette and with a few strokes—on the floor, on the wall, once on my pinafore!—there would appear a bird full of life and zip.

Father, as I said, had very definite ideas as to what was worth while and what was not. Though a true romanticist and a tender husband and father, he loathed sentimentality, he hated falseness, he detested show-offs. He could love a craftsman, a hedger, a ditcher, a wheelwright. I have seen him shake his head over a well-turned furrow, or a well-tied sheaf. "By the Lord Harry"—his favourite expression—"there's art for you!" He hated "gentility" and "refinement".—"No gentleman is refined," was one of his sayings.

He hated Mammon, and money was a forbidden subject. "I don't care a tinker's cuss" (we wondered what that was, but it sounded exciting) "I don't care a tinker's cuss if any of the family make any money or not—it's *doing* things that matter, and the best things aren't done for filthy lucre." Don't fear, Father, *none* of us have made any money.

He hated factory-made or ready-made things. We were not allowed to buy anything we could make. The result was we all learned to use our hands. Not in one way only but in many ways. We all made our own Christmas, birthday, and Easter cards; I still do. We all made our cowboy, Zulu or Indian costumes, and Father saw to it that they were made properly. It was not enough for me to make a war bonnet of turkey-tail feathers—I had to get down Catlin's *North American Indians* and choose whether I wanted to be a Blackfoot, a Pawnee, an Onendaga, or a Huron.

We did not know we were being educated in attention to detail, in proper handicraft methods, in the knowledge of people in distant lands—but we were.

We had our own orchestra, conducted by Mother, who wielded a strict baton. We played her orchestral pieces, as well as the not-too-hard classics.

We had our debating society, which discussed everything from growing peas to machinery's value to the Central African.

We had our police system: a judge, Mark, authorized to deduct fines from pocket money; prisoner's counsel, who was Philip and an executioner, Will, who could give us up to six whacks—over six was Dad's job. I must say, having been many times prisoner at the bar, I have no complaint so far as justice was concerned.

Do you see now why it was not hard for Mother and Father to raise us? We had to take on the responsibility of citizenship at an early date, and the Prime Minister did not have to do the civil-servant jobs. Nowadays it is just too bad if an elder brother tries to discipline a younger, for modern parents try to equalize all their children. Not so my father. "There is no such thing as equality," he would say. "Equality of opportunity, we hope; equality of accomplishment, of course not."

We never pestered our father for money—first, because we automatically got our penny or tuppence a week; secondly, because we knew if we wanted a thing badly enough we could make it. I mentioned this penny a week to a young lady of fourteen today (she would have been called a kid in 1912) and her remark was, "How on earth could you live on a penny a week?" I hate explaining the obvious, so forebore to point out that we no more had to "live" on our penny a week than she had to "live" on her generous allowance.

Of course, we were lucky—damn lucky. We had no radio to distract us and no "funny" papers to prevent us from reading and so allow our minds to rot. We had to delve into the works of Dickens and get a laugh out of the twist of his sentences and his joking words. Having earned our laugh, we enjoyed it the more. We had no car to take us away from our studies or hobbies. It never occurred to us to want one.

Father believed in getting information from source. Once he had to illustrate a book on ships called *Britain's Bulwarks*. The publishers chose Father because of his knowledge of ships of all riggings and centuries, and suggested that he might consult a certain reference book to refresh his memory. That was not good enough for Father. Off to Portsmouth he went for two weeks. I have some of his pencil sketches of block and tackle and hawser eyes today. They are priceless gems of craftsmanship.

I wanted to trap moles. Father found me reading about mole-trapping methods in a boy's outdoor book. "Don't just sit stuffily reading," he roared. "I'll have no dilettante amateur here. Off you go to old Crittenden and trap moles with him, or else you can weed the garden." You will have gathered we learned to take rebuke without sulking. "Thank you sir," said I and was off.

Talking about moles, my mother had a lovely moleskin jacket left to her by a rich sister. One day she said to Father, "Wouldn't a moleskin hat look nice with this—you know, one of those round flat-topped Russian things?" "Oh, Molly can make one," said Dad; and Molly did. I trapped the moles with three traps borrowed from old Crittenden, John skinned them, Jim tanned the skins, Betty got a pattern from a friend of hers and made up the silk lining, and Molly assembled the whole. It was our birthday present for Mother that year, and one and all voted it the most splendid piece of headgear ever turned out by the firm.

So, in this fashion, we found out what we wanted to know. We learned to make contacts. (It wasn't easy to ask Crittenden for traps —he was a crusty old boy!) And, above all, we learned to do things for others.

Father never started us on anything. If he helped us at all it was to finish a thing, and then chiefly by telling us how to find out the way to finish it. He never tried to save us from difficulties. He blandly saw us get into them and stood on the side-lines. I am sure he felt confident the training he had given us would come to our rescue, and usually it did. If a scheme failed he would say, "That's excellent—we build success on failure, you know." Another of his sayings was, "Of course, any decent man has enemies. Show me a man today, or in history—a man worth his salt—without enemies."

None of Father's children had what is called a college education. What was much more important, we learned how to take a bawling out, how to use horse sense, how to manipulate the most unpromising materials or disheartening conditions into lasting things of value. Summed up, how to live what they now call, I believe, "a full life." How to be happy on the half loaf, which is all most of us get out of life anyway—to the lasting good of our sense of humour and our immortal souls.

Father's system for raising his children was based on certain definite ideas which he put into practice. First, none of us were ever alone. We had no chance to sulk, to get moody or neurotic. Second, we were never unsupervised. I do not mean we were interfered with. We had to do things ourselves, but someone saw to it that we did them. Thus followed the third, automatically: we were never idle. Fourth, we were "taught" very little. Certainly we did not have to be bored with subjects like art appreciation or musical theory. That last was taken at the proper time and proper place by those of us who desired it. It was not taught to us as little children by a teacher who had been taught it out of a book by another teacher who wasn't a musician. We never heard of those subjects—but we loved music and art and after growing up knew what to choose.

Neither were we taught good manners—we lived them; nor grammar—we talked it; nor English literature—we read it.

I forgot to say that candy was rationed very strictly—more than two chocolates at a sitting made you a "pig." And we never got vitamin pills, orange juice, or crispy crunch, or pop-crackle-snap, or ice cream—and don't think those things didn't exist in those days, but they were considered trash. "Refined" people ate them—the *nouveaux riches*—not people of good family. George VI and his father got about the same treatment as us—cruel, wasn't it? In short, according to modern standards, we were frustrated, bullied, undernourished, and inhibited, to a point where it is nothing short of a miracle that we were not juvenile delinquents.

Perhaps now you can see why my father was one of the richest men in the world, and why I count myself the same. If you have a true sense of values, you are rich. As free-will beings, we can make our own choice; but there isn't much hope unless we are trained in what to choose.

We have to be just as careful about what we reject as what we retain. We can refuse God because we cannot prove Him. We can reject good manners because they are old-fashioned, and besides, it is "smart" to be rude. We can reject *The Decline and Fall of the Roman Empire* because it is easier to read a digest, and who bothers about the old Romans now—even though they still influence most of what we think and do. We can reject Chopin and Beethoven because it is such a bore to have to sit and listen; the radio is much better—you can play bridge, talk to your neighbour, and listen to boogy-woogy, all at the same time. We can reject handicrafts and the arts because, after all's said and done, you can get anything from a framed picture to a model of a horse at Eaton's. Finally, we can even reject having a family nowadays.

Well, add up all the rejections and you see why psychiatrists make a living—and the reasons behind a lot of our other social problems. You will also see why my father was rich even with bills staring him in the face, and why people with more money than they can spend are poor. And you will understand why I am as happy in the Peace River making a meal of porridge as I am on a holiday in New York facing a five-course dinner; enjoying the sound of a cowbell in my valley, or listening to an orchestra playing the *Messiah*.

11

Finally, my father was rich by virtue of a very old natural law, a law restated some two thousand years ago in the words, "give, and it shall be given to you." My father gave. He gave up fame and popularity as a well-paid society portraitist, to paint what he felt impelled to. You will see his works in the mosaics of Westminster Cathedral and in the Great Rood. Not being famous, he received just enough from this work to pay the butcher and the baker. He gave up "respectability" to have a large family, and reared them in a rambling old farm-house in Sussex, where there was room to swing a cat or a sword—but no sewer. He gave time, which he wanted for real painting, to do pot-boilers (and damn good ones) for the *Graphic*, the *Sphere*, and the other magazines, in order that his family would want nothing—and I mean *want nothing* that was necessary for their spiritual, bodily and mental health according to his mature and level-headed sense of values. According to present-day American standards we supposedly wanted everything; but you see we didn't know, we thought we were rich. We were, and are.

I am glad my father didn't live to see the Welfare State, or hear the spokesmen of security. He would have roared, "What the hell do they mean by security? We all have to die, haven't we? Where is the fun in life, where is the adventure, if you know everything is going to be all right next year?—which it won't anyway." Father did better than the State can ever do; he *built* security into each one of his children. He taught us the dignity of all and any work. He taught us to work for a pittance if need be and not envy the less capable fellow who was making the fortune. He taught us to rise above circumstances. To "walk with Kings—nor lose the common touch." To see our best work destroyed by boorish hands and yet take heart and rebuild. He taught us to forgive. Above all, he taught us to realize that because of God we could be as dead yet living, as scorned yet loved, as poor yet possessing all.

My father died when I was thirteen.

CATTLE TRAILS

CHAPTER TWO

Box Elder Ranch

"How much further?" I inquired for the fifth time. My companion flicked his whiplash at a gopher scurrying across the trail. "A ways, laddie," he said, as he had said four times before.

So I relapsed into silence, following the advice of the liveryman at Maple Creek. He had got me the job with Scotty, the grizzled Orkneyman who had left his native island so long before to join the Mounted Police at Fort Walsh, and now owned one of the best ranches in the Cypress Hills, as well as the livery barn at Maple Creek. I meant to keep this job if I could; and if the man's advice to keep my mouth shut and my ears open would help, why then I'd take it.

I hadn't much money when I hit Maple Creek—then, as now, a dry, dusty cow-town, but then with its outline unrelieved by trees and shrubbery, the wooden sidewalks ending abruptly at the edge of the prairie. The blue ridge of the Cypress Hills made a backdrop for the neat police barracks, over which the familiar old flag of my boyhood waved so bravely. No, I hadn't much money; and life, the prairie, those distant blue hills called me, and I wanted to see it all. And now, with a job already in hand, I felt I was well on my way.

We had been traversing the brown prairie since early breakfast, and now the sun was already hanging low over a great blue hill which I was to know as Eagle Butte. The monotony of the journey—and by monotony I don't mean boredom, but rather a drowsy sameness all quite delightful—had been broken at Fish Creek where we had made a noon camp to rest the horses and boil some coffee.

And the journey had been briefly broken on two other occasions, once when a rider in woolly chaps had stopped to parley, and once when we passed a sheep outfit on the move. Each time Scotty had brought the team to a halt and hailed them: "Hi there, are you frae Aberdeen?" The question seemed to be familiar, for the answer had been "Sure" in a pleasing drawl from the cowboy, and "You betcha" from the Basque sheepherder. Whereat Scotty leaned back over the democrat seat and lugged up the big jug of rye which reposed among ropes and blankets and sides of salt pork. And each in turn had taken a pull, holding the jug by a forefinger over the crook of the arm, Swedish style; after which the jug was tucked away and we drove on.

As we neared the hills the country became more and more rolling and the trail wound in and out following the draws. The creaking democrat splashed through shallow creeks and rattled over pebbly wash-outs, until finally we climbed out of a coulee to level, high prairie where the air was cool and sweet after the dust and heat we had trotted through all day.

My boss, a heavy, hearty man with a handle-bar moustache, handed me the reins. "Take the lines, Charlie," he said. (Most English greenhorns are called "Charlie" in the cow country.) With his stetson well over his eyes, he lolled back his head on the hard up-holstery, braced his feet against the dash, and fell asleep.

I took the lines, but did no more. The team—wiry, small-hoofed cayuses—had never swerved all day from the two tracks which made the trail, and I thought they were doing all right. So I simply held the lines away from their swishing long tails and left them alone.

Kip, on the right, was a strawberry roan with white legs and a broad blaze. His mate Bunco was a blue roan with some white patches that made him almost a pinto. Like all western horses they had long manes, tails, and foretops. Although not over fourteen hands, they had cheerfully eaten up over thirty miles of trail already.

As the sun began to slide down behind the hill, Kip and Bunco quite suddenly wheeled into a trail which met ours at a sharp angle and in another minute stopped before a barbed-wire gate with high posts, beyond which a group of weathered log buildings formed a sort of shapeless blur. Scotty woke up. "Open the gate," he said and took the lines. "We're home."

Putting the team away by lantern light with old Sandy, the collie, frisking at their heads, I saw for the first time a watering trough made from one solid cottonwood log, opened for the first time a swinging-pole corral gate, and smelt for the first time the sweet, herby scent of prairie hay as it was forked down from the loft above the log stable. I stood for a little while looking across the shadowy corrals where vague forms of horses moved, until I could see the bulky black shoulder of the butte against the starry sky.

Scotty touched me on the shoulder. "Supper," he said. "Come on or Ma won't like it." I followed in a sort of trance which was soon dispelled by the bright light of the oil lamp in the kitchen. The boss's wife, neat in a checked apron, was taking hot biscuits out of the oven of the Home Comfort. Coffee bubbled in a granite pot; on the well-scrubbed cabinet big, brown loaves steamed, belly upward, cheek by jowl with fragrant pies. On the table was a platter of smoking beef.

Scotty was already toweling himself, puffing noisily through his moustache, by the time I had taken all this in and been greeted. He indicated the wash-bowl and I dowsed my head and slicked my hair quickly, for I was hungry. "Make out your supper," said the boss. I did.

Box Elder Ranch squats beside McKay Creek, which flows around the shoulder of Eagle Butte; and Eagle Butte is the highest point in that long, narrow range called the Cypress Hills. Eagle Butte is in Alberta but the ranch lies just over the eastern boundary in Saskatchewan. From here the hills extend roughly thirty miles both east and west, so they can be claimed by both provinces. In the old days when Fort Walsh—just south over the hills—was the most important post of the North West Mounted Police, all this area was part of the Territory of Assiniboia.

To the north all is sere, rolling prairie extending across the South Saskatchewan and the forks of the Red Deer, over the rolling Coteau des Prairies to the great wheat plains of the Goose Lake country. Seen from the hills this presents an immense panorama in pastel colours, with occasional bright glimpses of lakes, over which the cloud shadows chase each other in endless play.

Immediately south is the steep north slope of the hills, heavily wooded with poplar and spruce on the lower levels and fringed with lodge-pole pine on their crests. A hay trail back of the corrals winds steeply up through the timber to the bench on top, where the pines end as abruptly as if the forest had been trimmed at that point with great shears. The level bench itself, close to four thousand feet above sea level, stretches endlessly east and west, covered with the thick, curly fescue called prairie wool and slashed by the heads of innumerable coulees.

In winter the fog comes down, on occasion so suddenly that a rider can depend only on his horse to reach his destination, and it is at this time that these coulees are most dangerous. The wisest horse, not being able to see more than its own length in any direction, may stumble into one and find himself completely helpless in the snow which has drifted full from bank to bank.

In summer the whole bench for miles puts forth a succession of flowers which are hard to match anywhere. Before the snow in the coulees has gone the higher ground is bright with the low-growing moss-phlox, which turns slowly from white to mauve, and which in its turn is followed by the prairie anemones, and later by the tall, graceful blue lupin, which sometimes covers acres. Everywhere above the 2500-foot level is the shrubby cinquefoil, which is reminiscent of gorse on the South Downs with its prickly leaves and yellow blossoms. Here, too, in summer you hear the wild sweet note of the upland plover and the little tinkling song of the Baird's sparrows.

But in the pine woods you leave all that behind and fancy you are in the North, for the crossbills creep about in the high branches and drop the trash of dead needles and cones all about you. Small birds that at first glance look like myrtle warblers will, if watched closely, disclose a bright yellow instead of a white throat, for they are Audubon's warblers.

Further down in the tangled coulees are the ruffed grouse, redstarts and MacGillivray's warblers, flickers and willow thrushes; while around the shining beaver ponds you hear the plaintive peep of spotted sandpipers, and perhaps glimpse a kingfisher as he rattles by. Around the ranch buildings the commonest bird is Say's phoebe, that rufous yellowish-red flycatcher so like in shape to its common small relative further east, but without the latter's nervous energy. And early spring finds the corrals and feeding-grounds invaded by mixed flocks of pink-sided juncos and tree sparrows, followed in May by the white-crowned sparrows, whose wheezy song—which reminds one so much of a yellow hammer—is heard every day and everywhere for several weeks.

Curiously enough, here in the hills is found also the cottontail rabbit, the only true rabbit of Saskatchewan, quite different from the long-legged plains hares and the varying hares, which we miscall snowshoe rabbits.

The south slope of the hills is quite different, being rugged and bare of trees except in the many coulees, which, like those on the north, generally harbour a flowing spring of clear water which gradually trickles down to help make the many creeks which drain the hills. The creeks that flow north empty into the prairie lakes, which in times of drought are apt to dry up altogether, so that the water never reaches any further. But those flowing south join up with larger creeks, which in turn join the Milk River, which meets the Missouri system, and the water eventually finds its way to the Gulf of Mexico.

South of the hills lie the great cattle ranges where so much riding has to be done. For a thousand head of cattle scattered over their wrinkled face are as lost as needles in a haystack.

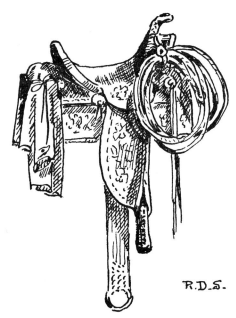

R.D.S.

We were in the big pasture of the old Box Elder Ranch, rounding up the brood mares in preparation for the branding of the foals. How the galloping of hooves stirred the blood! What more could a youngster ask for than the sweep of broken plain and sunny sky, the fragrant prairie wind on his cheek, and a willing horse between his legs?

With still three miles or more to go, the herd—which at first had run willy-nilly this way and that, as some old band leader strove to break away, only to be turned by the alert riders—was now deploying in something like order down the side of a steep boulder-strewn coulee. Still the pace was terrific. Clouds of dust spurned upward by flying hooves held the spicy smell of sage, and hung yellow in the sunshine. Anxious mothers whinnied to leggy youngsters, who checked in fright at the steepness of the drop. But the terror behind was greater than the fear in front, and urged on by the cries of the riders the little fellows hopped, skipped and jumped to the coulee bottom amid the cracking of brush and the click of hooves against stones, then with hardly a pause commenced the upward zigzag climb.

We riders had time to ease ourselves in the saddle and pass some chaff back and forth before we too tackled the deep V of the coulee. How I loved those downward rides! One last view of tawny uplands, one last waft of breeze on sweating face, and then the dip down to the hazy bottom. Buckskin picked his way with grunts of disapproval, his head free and reins slack so as not to interfere with his balance, then with a creak of saddle leather made the last slide to the cool bottom. A brief scanning of the opposite slope, and then he began to pick his way upward, pausing now and then to get his wind.

Once on the prairie level again, the riders brought the now scattered band to some semblance of order and headed them for the south-east, where a few miles away the weather-beaten corrals crouched against the drab earth at the foot of the hills.

The stiff pace began again, for the herd was still fresh, and in the manner of all wild mothers the mares tried to take themselves and their young to high ground. An old pinto mare, the leader of a small band of pintos of all ages, broke away to the left heading for a rock ridge.

I had been dreaming again, lulled by the drowsy drumming of Buckskin's hooves on the matted prairie. My mind had been busy with light and shade, colour and line; my eyes had strayed from the horse herd to the purple haze of the Cypress Hills.

A second is a lot of time when gathering range horses. My pony noticed the pinto break before I did, and swerved, bringing my mind quickly back to business. But we were a fraction too late and the pinto had the lead. Buckskin stretched himself and began to run in real earnest. The whole herd threatened to follow the pinto, but another rider shot forward to take my place on the flank and checked

19

them. Slowly Buckskin gained on the pinto, but still she reached the crest of the ridge ahead of us. She turned partly from her course and, followed by her band, took off down the length of the ridge. Strewn as the ground was with boulders and undermined with badger holes, it was not the safest place for a race. Going at a fool's pace, I felt Buckskin check in his stride for a fraction of a second, and thought —a snake.

In that second I glanced down and to the left. There on a bit of fine gravel, shadowed from the south by a limestone rock, were the eggs of a Sennett's nighthawk—those beautifully blotched twin eggs which are laid on the ground by a bird which makes no nest. Right in the open are they laid, and so closely do they resemble their surroundings, as does the bird herself when brooding, that they are as safe as in a thorn thicket. (Years after this, a bird of this same species laid its eggs on the bare concrete steps leading to the front door of the Legislative Buildings in Regina, and there safely hatched her young. And of all the hundreds of people who went up and down those wide steps daily, a bare dozen knew the bird's secret.)

How often had I looked for a nighthawk's nest, but always in vain, although I had more than once flushed a bird from what I felt sure was the near vicinity of its nesting site, just as Buckskin had flushed this one and let me know by flinching as her shadow caught his eye. For one brief moment my eye took in the picture of blotched ovals lying on their bed of matted gravel, the whole so clear cut that by shutting my eyes I can see them again. For a brief moment only, for Buckskin had not paused, and by the time my mind had taken in this one perfect view we were rods away, and the work went on.

It was not until the following Sunday, after the last of the foals had felt the X-Open-A brand on its velvety shoulder and had been nuzzled and comforted by its wild-eyed mother, that I was again able to visit the rock ridge. But in spite of diligent search and much backtracking of Buckskin's hoof marks, I was unable to find the eggs or see the bird. A buzzard far above wheeled and screamed, and Buckskin nosing the dry grass made metallic sounds with his bit, but the sun-baked rock ridge kept its secret.

About five miles north of Box Elder Ranch is a large butte which towers over the prairie like a Rock of Gibraltar; but it is rather clay than rock, an outcropping of what the geologists call the Irvine Pale Beds. Sloping gradually upward from the east, it rises to a summit some hundreds of feet above the general level of the plains. The top is almost flat, and the south, west, and north sides drop sheer to the plain again.

The butte is old—so old that on its exposed stratified face one can read the history of the days when the cool prairies were steaming swamps, and strange creatures like mediaeval dragons hunted through leafy aisles.

Years of buffeting winds and torrential rain storms have eroded its face, carving cracks and grooving wrinkles, playing havoc with its features as the years put the mark of age on human faces. All around is grassy prairie, with outcroppings of chalky clay where sage and cactus alone grow. These are the only plants which can find a foothold on the face of the butte, and even they are few and scattered near the steeper summit, and quite absent for the last hundred feet.

On this wind-swept height the lords of the surrounding terrain have made their homes for years. Ferrugineous rough-legged hawks, we call them, next in size only to the eagles and commonly called buzzards by the natives. For years on years, for uncounted decades, long before the memory of living man, these birds or their forebears have nested on this exposed cliff face, using a slight natural shelf as a site for their home.

The nest is a huge pile of sticks, largely sagebrush, but with an admixture of some willow and poplar twigs brought from Lord knows where—the accumulation of years, the layer next to the clay dry-rotted almost to a powder, and the bulk of the whole almost sufficient to fill a wagon box. The remains of other nests, almost as bulky but unused for years, still cling to former nesting-places. From this lofty eyrie the buzzards can scan the country for miles, and, by ascending a few hundred feet to hang in the upper air, can quickly enlarge the scope of their vision a thousandfold.

It was on a day in May that I first visited this butte. I had been told of the pair of buzzards nesting there, and soon saw them launch themselves from the face of the cliff. The climb to the ledge was no easy matter, but once accomplished was well worth the effort, and soon pencil and sketch-book came into play, to the great resentment of the guardian of the beautifully blotched eggs.

Dried portions of fur and bones bore witness to the useful activities of these birds as destroyers of gophers and other rodents, with never a feather to mar the record.

This was the first of several visits to the butte. On the last occasion I thrilled to the sight of the two old birds and three clumsy young of the year wheeling in squadron formation against a sky which held a threat of autumn storm. Until the time for southern migration the family clung together, and not a day but they could be discovered perched on cottonwood trees in the vicinity, or wheeling gracefully overhead, from which points of vantage they could make forays in pursuit of gophers or those smaller delicacies, grasshoppers.

But of the five, only four lived to travel the sky road when frost sered the prairie grass, for one luckless youngster, too confident in the family reputation for blamelessness so far as chickens were concerned, fell victim to a well-intentioned but uninformed "sportsman" who let fly at him with a charge of No. 5 shot. And he came to earth, never to see the warm sands and home-like buttes of Mexico, but to rot on the cold northern plain.

What a pity that man, possessed of the God-given power of reasoning, should in ignorance and wantonness take the lives of these, whose heritage is the arched blue of heaven by day, and the shelter of the clay wall by night!

CHAPTER THREE

Ma Parsons

MRS. PARSONS is about ninety if she is still alive—and I bet she is. She was young at eighty-six when I saw her last.

She is the mother of eight—not counting George who passed away as an infant. In more senses than one, Mrs. Parsons' kind never say die, and she is grandmother to about a baker's dozen. Only when she's telling you about it she says "a scattering."

I used to ride with her son Allen, who was older than I, and a thoroughly good cow hand. Sometimes I used to ride over to their ranch of a Sunday, and have a good feed—Allen always said his ma was a first-rate hand at pies.

I knew the family had come from the East years before, over the plains by wagon; and between yarning with Allen and asking questions of the old lady, I pieced together the story, which is a remarkable epic of pioneering, not so much for the adventures encountered, as for the lack of them.

She was born Rowena Webb, at Horning's Mill in old Ontario, in the days when it was Upper Canada and the third concession was 'way back in the bush.

She was seventeen when she married Amos Parsons, who had been her father's hired man; and like most young folks of those days, they planned for a farm of their own. So they went to Manitoba. "Manitoba was turrible far in them days."

Amos was from what they call pioneer stock, which means he wasn't afraid of work. If he *had* been he would never have been able to work for Tom Webb, let alone marry his daughter. Tom's own father had hewn out—yes, literally hewn out—a farm home from the hardwood bush. And this is almost precisely what his son-in-law did, for he chose a homestead in the wooded valley of Swan River in sight of the blue heights of the Riding Mountain; and granted that soft white poplar and bunchy willow fall to the axe more easily than maple and ash, still it took a worker to prove-up and get title.

But I won't go into details of grubbing willow crowns and urging the ox-drawn breaker plow through the heavy sod; of the building of the log shack; of the first crop of Red Fife wheat. Nor of Rowena's long winter evenings knitting for her growing family, or the equally long summer days of housekeeping, chicken rearing, and gardening.

Some day perhaps I shall, because in a raw young land, without servants and lacking municipal conveniences, these things are greater than they sound.

Neither shall I more than mention the many anxious nights when her man was late coming from "town," as they called the little settlement where the trading was done—nights when she sat up, keeping the kettle hot; straining her ears for the creak and whine of sleigh runners, but hearing only the hiss of the wind-driven snow as it banked against the cabin; hoping he would see the guiding rays of the lantern she had hung at the gate.

I want to tell you of Rowena's crowning triumph—The Trip, as she called it.

Well, after many years on the homestead, they made good; but as the farm became well established, more settlers came, and then the railroad; and presently, to use Rowena's words, "a person didn't have room to swing a cat any more." Amos, as I told you, was pioneer stock; and so was Rowena.

Amos got restless first.

"They say there's first-class cattle country 'way west; good grass and lots of room." A bit too dry for wheat; but he preferred cattle anyway. And he wanted to take a look at it.

So they talked it over. Amos wanted to take a look, and perhaps get work with one of the ranchers, and he figured Rowena could run the farm for a bit. Allen was thirteen now and could handle the plowing and cutting, and the littler 'uns could stook the grain and do chores. If he settled on a place she could come out later and bring the family and the stock.

Rowena, at sight of his glowing face, knew her man had already made up his mind. She belonged to a breed of wise women who know that there is a type of man who has to follow a star; and she had the loyalty as well as the love which goes with that breed. So she never for a moment even considered that there was anything else she could do but stick it out and leave him to go his way.

And so it was arranged.

Amos went to Swift Current, then the jumping-off place for the cattle country of what was then Assiniboia Territory. A year later found him herding cattle on Battle Creek, just south of the rolling Cypress Hills, where Canada touches the State of Montana among broken hills and scented sage flats.

To the south, sixty miles away, rose the jagged peaks of the Bear Paws, to the south-west the triple buttes of the Sweetgrass Hills, to the north the timbered coulees and level high benches of the Cypress. Towns? Havre, Montana, a wild cow town, forty-five miles to the south on Milk River. To the north-east, on the Canadian Pacific's transcontinental line, Maple Creek, a booming cattle town with its neat Mounted Police barracks. Neighbours? A few ranchers—Texans, down-East Canadians, English, and Scotch; a few Mounted Police-men and some half-breed horse breakers; plenty of half-wild range cattle, mustangs, antelope, and other animals of the plains.

Roads? Prairie trails—twin grooves a few feet apart, worn by freight wagons in the grassy sod, winding snake-like between the low hills and over the gentle swells.

A big land of immense blue distances and great horizons. A dry land, where grass is green only briefly in May and June, scorched to tawny and yellow and pinkish-grey in fall. A land of high plateaus and clear, crisp air; of balmy spring breezes and January blizzards.

But, as Amos had been told, a good cattle country—the very dry-ing of the grass on the stem being a curing process which retained in the blade all the nourishment that stock required for winter grazing.

Amos had filed on a quarter by the creek, and had a small log shack sheltered against a cut bank, a few good saddle horses, and a Cripple Creek saddle. With grazing plentiful, he had contracted to run a bull herd for the ranchers; so he had a few dollars coming in, and could see his way, as he would have said, to running a "spread."

So he sent for Rowena. He didn't bother her with details and in-structions as to what to sell and what to bring, or how to do it. He knew Rowena; so he simply wrote:

Dear Rowena:

I have started a ranch on Battle Crick. Sell the Farm or tell Lawyer Robson to sell it if you can't right away. Bring the cows and oxen and wagons and whatever you think we need. Allen better herd the cattle along. If you start the first grass you'll get here before freeze-up. When you get to Maple Crick go to Trueman's barn and he will put you on the Havre trail. Cross through the Cypress Gap and you will come to the Police post at Ten Mile, and the fellow there will show you the trail to our place, it's only a few miles further. Take care of yourself and take it easy, and tell the kids to be good.

Hoping this finds you and the kids fine as it leaves me, I sign myself as usual,

Your loving husband.

P.S. I should of said theys plenty of good spring water and some reel pretty flowers here, and you will like the place.

So Rowena sold the farm—there were plenty of buyers in those days, what with the new railroad and all—and set about the business of packing. This was April, and new grass meant about the end of May—plenty of time to get ready.

First to the bank, where she was told that a branch had been opened at Swift Current. So she had most of the money from the sale put through to Amos's credit there, carefully keeping enough for incidental expenses on the way. Pioneer women are good at business, even if they seem to handle it in a funny way sometimes—as when she parcelled up the notes and asked the bank manager to send them by registered mail to the branch out West. He smiled and said "Sure"; and Ma Parsons still swears that the identical notes of "my money" made the long trip!

Finances being shipshape, her next concern was what to take and what to leave. The big oval daguerreotypes of Pa and Ma, in their gilt frames, simply had to be taken; and great was her concern over the packing of this evidence of her good Ontario parentage. She dusted Ma's photo with great care, remembering the old lady's injunction about not packing dirty things.

Then there were the big cookstove, the heater, and the most substantial pieces of furniture; the chinaware, to be packed in barrels with the spare bedding; the kitchen utensils; and the special household treasures—especially the Good Book, in which were recorded her wedding day and the children's birthdays.

All the miscellaneous things, cleaned and sorted and packed, soon stood ready. The cookstove, the kitchen things, and the "using" bedding would be needed to the last minute, and had to be the last things loaded; and they would continue to be used on the way.

The two wagons were got ready. Tires had to be reset by the blacksmith, the wheels had to be well greased and the woodwork repaired. Two canvas tops had to be made, of heavy rough canvas that her sewing machine could not take; so she sewed them by hand, using an old sail-maker's palm that a sea-going uncle had given her for a souvenir when she was a little girl. Funny how things always come in handy if you keep them long enough!

Some of the older cows had to be sold and another strong ox bought, for old Muly was lame.

A month of methodical work—taking it easy as Amos had said—during which she was helped by thirteen-year-old Allen, who was coming into his growth, and rather hindered by the four smaller fry, two girls and two boys. A month of packing, figuring and planning, and all was ready.

The caravan—not an uncommon one in those days—left Swan River, Manitoba, on a May morning of bright sunshine that made the poplar leaves as yellow as the breasts of the meadow larks which fluttered and whistled before them.

Rowena drove the first white-canopied wagon, perched high on the spring seat and handling the heavy leather ox reins with ease—for they drive oxen like horses in Manitoba, with bridles and bits.

At the rear of the wagon she had set up her cookstove, its black pipe projecting through a neatly bound opening in the canvas, her flour barrel on one side of the stove and her pork barrel on the other; and here she cooked for six, three times a day. Rowena had wanted to bring at least one brood sow, but figuring it out she realized that the beast could hardly make it on foot with the cattle, and would take up too much room crated alive; and, as she said, "I like my pigs best in the pork barrel anyways." So that settled the problems of both transportation and of meat supply on the way.

Her utensils hung close to hand in friendly company, frying-pan and skittles clanking against each other with every jolt of the wheels. In this wagon, too, she kept the rolled-up bedding by day. At night it was spread on the wagon floor for her and the girls, and on the prairie grass under the wagon for the three boys.

The second wagon had the big hayrack on it, and was packed tight with furniture and hand tools. It also carried the cutting bar of a mowing machine, the wheel part of which was slung underneath. Here was a glorious miscellany of chattels, from the protesting hens in the crate at the back to the baby's cradle wedged in the middle, its interior crammed with winter clothing.

The quietest and oldest oxen were hitched to this wagon; and there being no one to drive them, they were simply fastened to the front wagon by strong halter shanks, which meant careful driving to prevent a sudden speed-up breaking the ropes.

Behind the second wagon and drawn by the simple expedient of having its shafts lashed to the wagon axle, came the shiny family buggy. Not for anything would Rowena have parted with that buggy. It was a symbol of prosperity and horsepower, marking the transition from the homesteader's oxen to the farmer's driving horses.

The one horse, a Standardbred driver, free of the shafts, carried young Allen as he brought up the rear with the driven cattle—eight or nine milch cows and a scattering of yearlings, heifers soon to be cows, and steers for the family beef.

That was the order in which the trip began, and that was the order in which they arrived at Battle Creek after traversing nearly seven hundred miles of scrubby poplar prairie, rolling plains, and rugged dry range lands.

The party travelled south-west for about two weeks, following the old Fort Ellice trail and crossing the Qu'Appelle River near Spy Hill. Then they proceeded westward parallel to the Canadian Pacific Railway, built only a few years before and still the only railroad in the whole North-West. Sometimes they were near it, sometimes far away, according to the trail; sometimes they came close enough to one of the string of mushroom towns to camp on the outskirts and do a little small shopping or have minor repairs made to the vehicles. Some days they travelled only seven or eight miles, on others ten or even fifteen; but not once did they move on a Sunday.

On the fine mornings all but the two youngest children—three-year-old Jessie and the baby, born after her father had left Manitoba—walked beside the wagons or else behind, helping Allen with the stock; sometimes running off the trail to look at a bird's nest in the grass, or pick the lovely harebells that nodded their blue heads all day. Their hard little feet, accustomed to being unshod in summer, scuffed the dust of the trail or scampered over prickly bull thistles with equal disregard.

On the rainy days, or when the strong west wind whipped the grasses low and sent dust devils whirling from horizon to horizon, Rowena made them stay under cover. Rain on a bare head, she averred, never did any good, and too much wind took the breath away.

And all the way across the plains this woman attended to her housework and chores in the same steady, orderly fashion that she had learnt as a girl.

With one exception—wash-day was not Monday but Saturday. I have already indicated that Rowena was no "Sabbath breaker" (as she would have said), and under no circumstances would she travel on the first day of the week. But she soon found that washing hung out to dry on and about the moving wagons picked up plenty of fine black dust, and that it would be necessary to stop and camp in order to dry the weekly wash properly; so she wisely altered the old family routine and washed at Saturday night's camp, hanging the clothes on a line between the wagons. And there they stayed all day Sunday, to be gathered clean and fresh as prairie herbs early on Monday morning.

She bathed the children first and washed the clothes afterwards, reheating the water in the big pot, as the children called the rotund and heavy cauldron which had started life boiling maple sap in the far-off bush days.

Sunday morning saw neat, clean children in a neat camp, gathered round their mother as she read from the Bible—stories of wanderings in strange lands, of hunger and thirst and deliverance—while the row of small garments flapped bravely on the line, and the oxen lay down with contented grunts to chew their morning cud.

"It didn't hardly look right," says Rowena, "to be reading from Scripture with the kids' underwear a-flapping; but anyhow *I* knew them clothes hadn't been washed on a Sunda, and I weren't going to take them down on a Sunda."

So Mrs. Parsons combined Sabbath-keeping with convenience and set her conscience at rest.

After three weeks or more of travelling over the park-like prairies to the Qu'Appelle, they began to leave the poplar and willow groves behind and come into more level and open plains. They missed the friendliness of the groves and they missed the hundreds of shining sloughs with their throngs of wild-fowl—green-headed mallard, graceful pintails, broad-billed shovellers, various small teal, and the black-and-white scaup ducks.

The grass began to get shorter and finer—real prairie wool—and they began to see birds which were strange to them—small black ones with white wing patches, which the children at once called white-wings, not knowing that they were lark buntings.

It speaks marvels for Rowena that somehow she always had a bright fire in her stove, and water in the barrel lashed to the wagon's creaking side. It also speaks well for the men—and the few women—that she met on the trail. Word always seemed to go ahead that a woman and kids were on their way West, so that sometimes when Rowena asked at a homesteader's sod shack or a constructor's camp as to the best place for water or grass, she found that she was already expected, and so had leave to camp by someone's well; or she might be directed to a creek or a spring.

When the scanty waterside willows permitted, the smaller children were set to work gathering dry twigs and branches; but otherwise their fuel was dried dung picked up on the prairie—"cow chips" as they called them, and mighty good fuel as every old-timer knows.

In the evening the cows had to be milked and the warm milk set

in pans overnight for the cream to rise. In the morning she skimmed it off and gave what was left to the calves—two of which had been dropped on the way, and were now crammed somehow into the second wagon. In addition, the morning's milk went directly to them—or at least as much as they could take. What the children and the calves could not drink had to be thrown away, as the cream would not rise during the daytime traveling.

"It seems a wicked waste," Rowena said to Allen, "but it can't be helped; and it spoils a good cow not to milk her twicet a day."

Her faithful barrel churn hung at the wagon's back, and twice a week the cream was put in it and turned to yellow butter by the ceaseless jolting and swaying of the wagon as it followed the uneven trail; so that at the evening camp it could be worked in the wooden bowl, salted, and pressed away in the big stone crocks.

As the July heat ripened the wild strawberries and saskatoons, there was many a feast of fresh fruit and cream to vary the monotony of salt pork, bread, porridge, and prunes. To smell that home-made bread and see that firm butter was almost as good as eating it; and what with a few eggs from the hens and plenty of thick cream on the breakfast oats, I can tell you from experience that Queen Victoria herself fared no better.

Not that things always ran smoothly. Like when the cows drifted off one stormy night and Rowena and Allen had to thrash about in the wet till daybreak rounding them up—only to find that in their absence Jessie had walked in her sleep, upsetting the sponge for the next day's bread and putting the whole camp in an uproar. Or when the baby got those bad attacks of croup which frightened her mother and kept her up nights, even though she knew croup sounds worse than it usually is.

And there was something close to loneliness to fight, for a grown woman yearns for somebody more "talkable" than a thirteen-year-old, and a boy at that; and some of the nights were very dark, and the coyotes' howling didn't make them any better.

Some nights she would wake with a feeling that something was wrong, and reaching out her hand would touch the rough side of the wagon box, and suddenly remember that she was out on the lone prairie with her small children dependent on her. But remembering Allen, almost a man, heartened her, and she would sometimes call out, "Are you awake, son?" and Allen would sleepily answer that he was, and add: "Go to sleep Ma, everything is all right, and I'm keeping Jim covered."

Then she would thank God for her sons, and cheerfully ask the Lord to see them safe through, and drop to sleep again to the familiar barn-yardy sound of the ox-bells tinkling in rhythm with the endless cud-chewing, while the frogs carried on their nightly serenade—"cree, cree, cree" from the little green ones, "ko-ruck, ko-ruck" from the old bullfrogs. Rowena always declared that when all the frogs stopped singing at once—as they sometimes do—the silence was the lonesomest thing.

Mosquitoes were a plague. On still evenings they appeared in grey clouds in the long grass around the sloughs and drove the stock almost frantic at times, as well as attacking the humans. The children's legs looked quite "measly," as they laughingly told one another. But as the dryer weather and the party's arrival into the shorter grass of the cattle country thinned the humming ranks of these insects, the party got respite and were gradually able to discontinue the smudge-pot of cow chips and green grass, and the children could stop scratching their legs.

Rowena herself, always a handsome woman, was burnt as brown as as any Indian, which showed off her white teeth and glossy hair. ("I mind the time I could sit on my hair.") But all resemblance to an Indian was lost when you saw her blue eyes, all etched around even then with tiny lines from squinting through sun and wind to the far blue horizon.

Nowadays, plenty of women think they can't be outdoors without dressing like men—slacks or men's shirts, and so on; but not Rowena. Coloured house dresses for her—washable, and kept washed and ironed. She wasn't going to look a fright even if she hadn't a home. A good bonnet, good button boots and decent black stockings, and the brooch Amos had given her one birthday pinned at her throat.

And a good nightdress for sleeping. She shared her mother's horror of being found improperly attired in case "something happened in the night."

They rose early and breakfasted early. But by the time the cows were gathered and the milking done and everything packed, it was usually about eight o'clock before they were off. Oxen are no good in the heat of the day, so they made noon camp about eleven o'clock, and while the oxen rested and grazed, Rowena would iron or mend or sometimes take a nap, while the elder children looked for berries. At three in the afternoon they would be on the trail again till six, when it would be time to make the night camp.

So they travelled on as spring gradually turned to summer, and the prairie became bright with sunflowers; and summer itself began to age, and the grasses ripened with the smell of new-mown hay; and the young gophers could be seen almost as big as their parents as they peeped and whistled from their holes; and floppy young buzzards screamed overhead and tried to wheel as gracefully as the old ones.

Suns rose like molten discs from behind the horizon's rim. Day breezes freshened and swept the grass into waves and ripples, and blew the brown pipits before the wagons like autumn leaves. After a morning's run, the children loved to lie back in the buggy and watch the procession of great fleecy clouds with turreted tops like castles, slowly and steadily moving overhead. Suns set slowly, gloriously, as only on the plains they can; cool nights followed burning days and sage-scented twilights.

And this woman, with her little world for which she was responsible, went on to where her man waited.

Cook, housekeeper, teamster, stockman; doctor, nurse, preacher, dairymaid—such was Ma Parsons. And doing all this in a perfectly natural, contented and efficient manner that left no room for stupid anxieties or useless grumbling.

She knew that she could hurry along and make the trip in little more than half the time. But she also knew the cost to the cattle, the vehicles, and her own nerves (though she wouldn't have understood *that* word!) of hurrying and bustling and being impatient. And she reckoned to arrive with the "hull kit an' boodle" safe and sound.

So it was well into August before they got to Maple Creek. There Trueman took care of their animals for a day or two, while his missus took care of Rowena's youngest children, so that Rowena herself could do a little shopping at Dixon's store and generally freshen up before starting on the last lap. And since one of the young policemen was making a patrol to Ten Mile, Trueman—who was well acquainted with the police through supplying fodder for their horses—asked him to let Amos Parsons know that his wife and kids had arrived from Manitoba.

So it came to pass that, having been duly put on the Havre trail by their friend, they were making noon camp at Fish Creek when Amos himself rode up.

33

And they were all happy, of course, and talked all together, and the baby was frightened of her father, but they finally got settled down; and in the evening, talking more quietly as the children slept, Rowena may have told Amos about the nights she was a bit scared. And she was proud to show him that she had made enough butter to do them all winter in case the cows dried up with the cold weather. And knitted a full supply for everybody of winter socks and mitts and scarfs.

She did like the ranch, and soon set about making the cabin more homelike. And they prospered as they deserved, in cattle and land; but better than that, they had three more children.

And Mrs. Parsons became Ma to most of the bachelors for miles around, though she was no older than most of them, and could trip it at the cowboy dances with the best,—yes, and make the finest coffee afterwards, while they all waited till daylight to go home.

When I last saw Ma Parsons, not so long ago, she sat in her big rocking-chair on the ranch porch, as happy and hearty and as full of fun as ever.

Allen, a great hulking chap with rough red whiskers, himself the father of four or five, had stopped in as he was riding by, and clanked through the kitchen, and had to be spoken to by his mother, who "never could abide spurs in my house."

He leaned down to kiss her and got another rebuke for not being shaven. "As sassy as ever, aren't you Ma?" grinned Allen.

I would hardly dare call Mrs. Parsons a heroine. She wouldn't like it. She thinks a "heroeen" is some woman who does something extraordinarily brave and marvellous.

And she only did what hundreds of woman (not all pioneers, either) have done. She kept up her end and stuck by her man—who, I forgot to tell you, was just as good at keeping up *his* end; and it's because of such as they that the world is as good and decent as it is. And because of such as they, too, that the prairies were all tamed and settled, so the newlyweds of today have their electric stoves and running water—with all the petty aggravations they cause!

No, I wouldn't call Ma Parsons a heroine. But I've had the honour of taking off my hat to her, and I do it again now; for she is as sassy as ever, because, as she loves to say, "Work never killed anybody yit."

CHAPTER FOUR

Valley of Gold

THE OLD outfit that had used the Arm River country for summer range had pulled out, fearful of the tide of settlement and restricted by the cancellation of their leases. However, there was still a considerable area of broken country which both the homesteaders and the railways had shunned. I knew it fairly well, and when I got the offer of good pay to run a summer herd there, I figured—and rightly—that this small range would still be good for a few years; at all events until the homesteaders had plowed most of their land, and their need for additional hay and grazing should drive me out. In any case I wanted to try something on my own which, if not quite so sure as forty a month and grub, held promise of some excitement.

The Arm River country is rough and rolling, crossed with old buffalo trails, its turtle-back hills interspersed with deep, grassy-banked sloughs. Through the heart of these hills the Arm River—scarcely worthy of the name here—meanders through a shallow valley perhaps three-quarters of a mile wide into which the higher ground pushes many rounded shoulders.

As I said, the heart of this area had been pretty well bypassed by the homesteaders, that flood of settlers seeking prairie lands to plow for wheat growing. This flood had spread far and wide and had long since engulfed the better-watered long-grass prairies of Manitoba and eastern Saskatchewan; but from the ranchers' point of view they were welcome to all that, for there the snowfall was too heavy, and the winters too bitter, for range stock. Also the grass did not cure well enough, and the chinook lost its strength and did little more than glaze the deep snow, making it even harder for stock on the range to reach the herbage; and therefore those prairies never had been cattle country.

But on the shorter-grassed plains further west, the feeling was bitter. It was the old story of the settler, who longed to own no matter how few acres, *versus* the grazier, who was content to use and share and had no desire that his personal boundaries be staked out and surveyed; the old problem of the apparently progressive opposed to the conservative.

The ranchers knew that much of their rugged range lands lacked the necessary rainfall for continued grain growing, while at the same time being eminently suited for stock raising, and therefore quite naturally felt that any encroachment upon their holdings by "dirt farmers" would benefit nobody—and said so. But their voice was hardly heard against the loud clamour of the land seekers. So the flood raced on—English and Scotch, Scandinavians, Germans, whole colonies of Russians, with a good scattering from south of the line. The land offices hummed, and claim to many a quarter section was filed sight unseen.

A great wedge of settlement had been driven between the southern ranges and the railroad, another one north of the river on the Goose Lake line, and still another further north. Except for the great cattle country of the Cypress Hills and Milk River, only the wrinkled Coteau remained as an isolated range—although even here the great Matador outfit was gone, replaced by smaller ranches. Elsewhere a few smallish islands of difficult country, such as the Arm River region, alone remained untouched by the hand of the farmer.

In cool April we had freighted in with three four-horse outfits and led saddle stock. The snow still lay in soggy drifts in the lee of the hills and the trail was soft and boggy in the draws. Sand-hill cranes were going through their weird spring dances on the knolls. Wedges of ducks passed overhead, while godwits, willets, and killdeer plovers clamoured about the sloughs. The curly grass, bleached white by winter, formed a dimpled and woolly mat which delayed the thawing of the ground on the northern slopes, where the wagons bumped and rumbled noisily.

Our headquarters were to be a few hundred yards up a side coulee which opened its wide mouth into the river valley. Here by a flowing spring we put up a small frame shack with the lumber we had brought,

and within it stacked our summer's grub supply. Next, a saddle-horse stable and a large herd corral, for the cattle would have to be confined at night owing to a few five-acre patches of crop scattered here and there within four or five miles' distance; and we certainly did not propose to night herd.

It used to gall us to think of thousands of acres of good range all around us ruined for free grazing by these wretched little patches that the homesteaders would not fence—or if they did, so inadequately that no self-respecting range cow would be discouraged, especially at harvest time when the binder chucked the meager sheaves right against the wire.

There was also a catch pen for branding, and for holding or roping out saddle stock.

I left one man there after the corrals were finished, to take care of things and run a fence around a few hundred acres to make a "wrangle field" (pasture) for our twenty-odd head of saddle horses. Then my helper Fred and I went for the cattle.

It was on the afternoon of a June day that Fred and I pushed the herd down over the steep hills into the valley, some three hundred head of cows and calves with a few steers and yearlings. As they smelled water they spread out and broke into a faster walk, the heat-drool from their jaws hanging in the air like cobwebs.

"Look at them flowers!" said Fred, and we paused and looked. Where in April the valley below us had been sere and brown with dead and rustling herbage, it now gleamed yellow and bright for its full length in the evening light. To the height of a rider's knee, wild sunflowers rippled in full bloom and bent to the cattle's flanks as they crowded to the water, from which frightened ducks rose in clouds. Our ponies pushed the plants aside with strong shoulders, grateful for the brushing away of mosquitoes from their legs and flanks; blowing through their nostrils to clear away the pungent pollen; sometimes pausing to nip at a yellow blossom.

Except when tormented by gadflies or drifting before a cold, lashing rain (what misery to sit in the saddle all day soaked through one's slicker!), the cattle usually bedded down soon after noon as we quietly circle-rode.

Sometimes when all was quiet and we knew the cattle would stay put for a while, we raced to a pool in the valley, stripped ourselves and our ponies, and rode into the cool water until the horses—who loved it as much as we—were swimming. Then we would slip from their backs and let them make their way to shore for a mouthful of grass while we disported ourselves.

On one occasion the ponies decided to go home and started off, holding the trailing lines to one side, as cow ponies do, so as not to step on them and jerk their mouths. Seeing this, Fred and I raced naked after them; but they began to trot, and we were a quarter of a mile from our clothes when Fred shouted, "Duck!" Turning, I saw what he saw—a buggy-load of young ladies, spanking down the prairie trail not two hundred yards away. We threw ourselves into the tall sunflowers and kept as still as mice until they had passed, in spite of the prairie needles.

By six o'clock in the evening the old herd leaders—foremost among them Grey, the outlaw steer—would begin to graze toward home. Slowly the younger stock followed and soon the whole herd would gather, and by force of habit walk in several files along the winding trails they had made, all of which spiderwebbed out from the main corral gate, till all were within and the gate shut; which meant supper for us about eight.

After days in the hot fly-time, when cattle stampeded in small bunches over the prairie and we had to ride so much to keep them out of the crops that we sometimes changed horses three times a day, it was a delight to follow the homeward herd along the valley's lower edge, with the purpling hills to the west and the golden sea to the right.

38

I've seen parks and gardens on two continents designed to show off all varieties of gorgeous blooms, but no such elaborate planning ever made me catch my breath as did this golden valley with its silver pools in its setting of low, treeless hills. Perhaps, of all the people who rode, or homesteaded, or worked in that district, I got the most happiness out of that valley—and I didn't own a thing but my saddle, my horses, and a few cattle running in the herd.

One hot September day found me riding west of the Saskatchewan River towards the Coteau. I had left the herd on Arm River in charge of the help and was heading for Bulliver's ranch, a small spread on the old Matador range.

My purpose was twofold. Some of my horses had strayed and I had found where they crossed the river, and their recovery offered a good excuse for a few days' holiday and a chat with Bulliver.

Noon found me eating hotcakes and bacon with him, but before the meal was finished a half-breed rode up to say the prairie was on fire on the other side of Tomlinson's, and everybody was turning out to fight it.

"All right, Delorme—thanks," said Bulliver as the man swung his horse and spurred away. "Better get our horses"—to me, pushing back his plate; and we hastily saddled up.

My strayed horses would have to wait.

The few ranchers who strove to maintain a foothold on the edge of the wrinkled plateau known as the Coteau des Prairies had overcome the successive epidemics of blackleg and the depredation of the "lopers," the grey wolves of the plains. They had stemmed the tide of dirt farmers who strove to drive their plows into the very heart of this range, and it looked as if their herds would be allowed to increase in peace. Now out of the West had come this enemy—an enemy which, if allowed to spread unchecked, would wipe out not only the hay they had stacked for winter feed, but the very grass of their pasture lands.

We gathered at Tomlinson's ranch to talk it over. There was Tomlinson himself, a lean-thighed Texan who used to be with the Matador people. There was Bulliver, an Englishman like myself, but much older and wiser in the handling of range matters. There were Swainson and Moen, Swedish partners from Dakota; Delorme, the half-breed horse rancher; Frenchy, and myself. Frenchy was a huge, unlettered French Canadian, whose given names, Louis Philippe, were as aristocratic as his demeanour and voice were *habitant*.

For days the smoky air had been redolent of sage and prairie herbs, and it choked us as we feverishly plowed fireguards.

Every dweller of the range land knows the anxiety suffered by all in a dry season, and this season was plumb hell. Day after day the sun stabbed down and curled and dried the grass a little crisper. Night after night the same sun went down swimming in a great gold sea, promising us only another blistering day to follow. Hot, dry chinooks fanned the overheated prairie day after day, obscuring the blue horizon in wave after wave of shimmering heat.

More than once we had been alarmed by the dancing dust devils because of their likeness to smoke plumes, and rarely did we permit ourselves the luxury of smoking, and then only when resting in the shade.

No one knew how the fire started—no one ever does—and therefore no one could be blamed. It might have started in one of a dozen ways other than carelessness; and no one in that country dares to be careless. Travellers, used to the safety of the city, have started terrible fires by throwing out the ashes of a pipe or the stub of a cigarette; but this country is rough, very rough, with only a few winding prairie trails, and travellers avoid it. It is more likely that one of the careful local people accidentally started this fire. I myself started a fire once when I thought that I was taking every precaution.

Riding one hot dry summer's day, I craved a smoke; for a long time I resisted, but eventually gave in. I smoked the way we do on the range. Walking my horse, I rolled my cigarette, hunched my shoulder to the wind, and with cupped hands lit up; then I carefully extinguished the match with my fingers and put it in my pocket. Still letting my horse walk, I kept both cupped hands around the cigarette to make sure that no ashes fell. Upon finishing the cigarette, the procedure was to spit in the palm of the left hand, drop the butt into it from the lips, and with the right hand squash and roll it to a nice messy pulp, finally dropping the resultant pellet into the pocket.

I had done this hundreds of times, often in a high wind. On this occasion, however, I had no sooner lit the cigarette than my horse stumbled into a badger hole, giving me such a wrench that the cigarette flew off into the grass; and before you could say scat a plume of smoke spiralled upward, the grass was so dry. Of course I jumped off my horse and beat the fire out in a few seconds.

And so, as I said, this fire might have started in one of many ways, but that did not matter very much just now. What did matter was that property was threatened and we had to do something.

Tonight the crooked skyline flushed red on three sides, and there was no sign of rain. We joined forces and fought like mad for two more days. Half the range was gone now, but we had managed to save the hay, except for a few stacks of Tomlinson's which had been burnt the first day, and the main fire was checked.

All that now lay threatened by crackling flames was the stacks on Frenchy's ranch, which lay furthest to the south, and it was on the third day that our little party set out for that place with two "stag" breaking ploughs drawn by skittish bronco ponies.

More than once the last two days we had urged Frenchy to take a couple of men and one of the ploughs and get busy on the protection of his own stacks; but always he had expectorated hugely and with his smoke-blackened face cracked into a grin, answered that since his ranch was furthest from the danger it could wait, and that in working with us he was best protecting his own.

Now that our side, the north, was safe, he suddenly became all anxiety and pushed his sorrel impatiently ahead, turning back often as if to hurry our progress with the ploughs.

At noon, topping a hogsback ridge, we could view the grassy valley which sheltered Frenchy's humble cabin, and down the centre of which were reared his neat stacks. And up the valley from the west, fire was raging before a freshening breeze. We were too late!

Slowly we straggled forward to the hill's edge, where Frenchy, dismounted, stood dully watching the imminent destruction of his holdings. His gaunt sorrel nosed the tinder-dry herbage uneasily.

Frenchy turned towards us. And we, who had witnessed his herculean struggles of the past days, looked away, but not before we had seen the tears which ran down his cheeks and left white furrows in the smoke grime.

Then Frenchy did something which perhaps more than one of us would have done had we had the courage and the faith. He dropped his bridle rein and fell to his knees on the sun-baked prairie, and with his bewhiskered face turned to the blue sky, and his arms extended upward and outward, he prayed; not the Paters and Aves learned at his mother's knee, but simple, strong words in his own broken English:

"Seigneur, you know me. My name ees Louis Philippe. Ees not good mans, me. Lots tam you hear me mak de bad words; bot Seigneur, ees brak de bronco, man forget wat hees spik. Oh, Seigneur, sure you seeing leetle picture 'Sacré Coeur' ees hang on my house? S'pose I forgetting mak some *prière* som tam, I know you not forgetting me. Nevaire before ees asking you som'ting, Seigneur, bot ees asking now. My name ees Louis Philippe, and I ask for you save my hay. I don' know how ees going do dat, bot you knowing how Seigneur.

"Ees makin best *prière* lak I nevaire do before; and now I got no more tam spik wid you for ees *beaucoup travail* for me, bot I tank you Seigneur, you helping save my hay now."

I shall never forget the scene. The rugged hills around us, the grass bleached tawny and white by the September sun, the fire advancing up the valley with the steady march of a red-coated regiment, the burly French-Canadian in the age-old attitude of supplication.

For a second the drama had appeared ludicrous, almost indecent in its naked frankness. But as the kneeling figure spoke on it was as if some old prophet were beseeching his Lord, and memories of lessons and readings crowded one's mind.

After all, were we not all akin to those tribes who had wandered for forty years in the desert? They too had known the long night vigils over their herds, when the calves were coming and the grey wolves were abroad. They too had battled against the desert and against disease.

They had been largely an unlettered people, but they had possessed an unbounded faith in their Lord, and their leaders had been wont to call on Him when encompassed by difficulties.

Frenchy rose to his feet. The dullness had left him, and his old energy had returned. "Queek, you fellers, bring dat plough, ees going mak fight lak hell now!"

Tomlinson muttered to me, "It can't be done, but we sorta have to make a stab at it after that." And so, with a will, we set to, leaving the row of stacks nearest the fire to take care of itself, while we endeavoured by coaxing, cursing, and straight hard whip-work to urge the broncos across the valley with the shares sunk deep, so that we would have a chance to back-fire.

Half blinded by smoke, and crazed with the heat of the crackling flames, the animals balked again and again. Leading, driving, pushing, wrenching at the wretched beasts, we saw each other only through a reeking haze, and it is still a wonder to me that no one was trampled underfoot in the melee.

All at once our shoutings and the gruntings of the broncos were drowned by the low rumbling roar of thunder. We looked up, panting.

The sky was darkening where only moments before Frenchy had raised his face to fairest blue. And as we looked the sun was covered, the breeze dropped, and on our upturned, sweating faces, moisture of a cooler nature pattered like a caress.

How sweet the feel of rain can be!

The very ponies stood quietly or shifted easily in their harness, no longer wide-eyed and round-nostrilled.

In less than ten minutes the drizzle became a downpour; and leaving the ploughs thrown on their sides, like deserted cannon on a battlefield, we jumped astride the broncos and raced for Frenchy's cabin.

While he regaled us with hot tea and hastily fried flapjacks, we were strangely quiet. No one felt like discussing the afternoon's happenings. Smoking after the meal, we would saunter one at a time to the window to look through the steady downpour at the haystacks in the valley. There they stood, no longer threatened.

Frenchy's Herefords would be full-bellied the coming winter, for the rain had damped down the fire at the very edge of the first stacks.

The wild-horse roundup was on. Orders had been given that the wild mustang ponies of the southern ranges be destroyed, for the grass they ate could fatten steers and they added to other depredations by luring into their herds the domesticated stock of the farmers and ranchers. The old range was passing and with it, we thought then, the old ways and the cattlemen. Ranchers now had to lease their grazing and every blade of grass counted.

So the roundup was organized, and the riders went out keen with the excitement of the chase; but not without a qualm on the part of some who cherished love for the wiry animals, and who came near to turning back at the thought of feeding them to foxes. (For the plan was to transform the pony carcasses into concentrated meal for sale to the fur farms, and actually most of the horses were shipped East alive and slaughtered there.)

The first band was sighted in the broken hill country near the Old-Man-on-His-Back, but the long-tailed grey mare that led them had been hazed before and she put all her speed, endurance, and plains wisdom into keeping her band together and eluding the riders as they closed in. Well in the lead, the grey would dash through the narrowing cordon with her following of younger mares and foals thundering behind, and head for the wilder gullies and badlands of Milk River.

One such break-away took the band so close to old Oscar Martinson's sheep camp that the silly bleating woollies dashed confusedly in all directions; and to a rider following on a sweat-crusted pony, old Oscar barked that the Government should pay a bounty on cowboys —not on wild ponies that minded their own business. The rider answered that the Government thought it more humane to corral and shoot the mustangs than leave them to starve to death on a stinking sheep range. Words had come perilously close to blows by the time the roundup foreman cantered up and put a curt stop to the conversation as he directed the work in hand.

All through the late summer and into the hazy blue fall the work went on, until the ranges from the Cypress Hills to the Montana line had been combed.

At the central camps creaking chuck-wagons sent up their blue smoke columns as riders came and went—some to roll in their blankets for a few hours' sleep, some to swallow hot coffee and snatch at bacon and biscuits before mounting stiff-legged to lope away again, some to tend bruised shoulders or sprained ankles resulting from falls on the badger-pocked ridges.

Dust clouds on the horizon showed where horses were being bunched and driven; and over the gathering-corrals a golden haze swam in the sunshine above the milling hooves of the frightened beasts. Of the work of taking them to the railroad and loading them in cars I do not care to write, except to say that many a near-broke cowboy dug deep into his dusty overalls to redeem from the rendering vat a striking pinto or roan which appealed to his fancy.

The wild and semi-wild ponies of the Canadian prairies are the same stock as the mustangs which range the dry belt southward to Mexico and west over the high sage waste of Nevada, Idaho and Oregon. Their common ancestors were the Spanish Conquistadors' horses, whose descendants increased untended for so many years until the Comanches tamed them. The ponies were brought to Canada by the Crows, the Gros Ventres, and the Blackfeet; and so eventually they came to the Crees, sometimes by trade and often by theft.

Although centuries of inbreeding and of facing bitter blizzards in winter have made them smaller and stockier, the wide nostrils, silky manes, large liquid eyes, and flexible pasterns still show the Spanish-Barb-Arab blood which is their heritage.

Hardy, wiry, and sure-footed, sleek as seals in summer and shaggy as bears in winter, they thrive on the short dry grass. For this is a limestone country, and if we ask why good horseflesh comes from Ireland, from New South Wales, and from Kentucky, one answer is —lime.

Winters of rustling through deeply drifted snow for the herbage beneath has given them great muscular development and the ability to make the best of a few mouthfuls. On bitter nights a band will stand head down and rumps to the wind in the sparse shelter afforded by a few creekside willows or a crumbling cut-bank; but before daylight comes they will move in single file to some hitherto ungrazed slope. There, under the leadership of a grizzled old matriarch, they recommence the never-ending task of pawing away the snow to graze—six paws with one forefoot, and a mouthful of grass; one step forward and repeat the process. The whole band faces one way and works in unison until satisfied. If the noon sun sends any warmth, they rest and doze, with little movement except for an occasional shifting of weight from one hind hoof to another, or a quick scanning of the horizon on the lookout for danger.

In very bitter weather, with the thermometer hitting the minus thirty's and forty's, I have been able to ride quite close to such bands by allowing my horse to proceed at a walk. The wild bunch would stand all to attention with ears pricked forward and their breath rising in the frosty air like smoke from so many fires. Sometimes after I passed they would commence to follow, overcome by curiosity; but to turn in the saddle was enough to send them plunging off with frightened snorts.

I was thinking of these things as I sat on a corral fence after the roundup. The cowboy who was fixing a saddle cinch nearby was saying, ". . . the best I ever rode was a buckskin from Milk River, but these yere pintos and blues and strawberries are all right purty; ain't they now?"

I said, "Yes, Pete, they are the most beautiful animals I have ever seen; and I was just thinking how much we owe these ponies of the West, because in the early days it was a big country to cover on foot. Even if their day is done, some of us—you and I anyway, Pete—won't forget them."

And Pete—whose grandmother, a daughter of the dons, had ridden beside her Texan husband up the cattle trails to the North-west, whose father had decided to stay in the cold North, Pete of the soft voice and hard body—answered, "Why now that's just what I was thinking. Say—anyways, I'm kinda glad Old Grey's bunch got away into the breaks."

I looked at him. His eyes were on the cigarette he was rolling. "You wasted a lot of time at old Oscar's sheep camp," I reminded him.

CHAPTER FIVE

Riding the Range

WHEN YOU think of a ranch, you probably think of whole herds of cattle, and possibly of horses too; but you may be on a ranch for some time before you see anything more than the saddle stock and the milch cows, and a good deal longer before you see a herd. You will see that only at roundup time or when cattle are being moved.

Actually there are very few cattle to be seen about any cattle ranch in summer—that is, anywhere near the buildings. Most of the level valley land nearby is used for hay, and is fenced around so that the crop is not spoiled by grazing. The open grass land adjoining is generally fenced off for winter range—the term winter field is now the correct one, even if the area contains thousands of acres.

So in order to see cattle in any number you have to ride the range, and even then you may be very disappointed if you have been told that the ranch runs, says, two thousand head of cattle. In a day's ride—especially if you don't know where to look—you may see only forty or fifty, and these won't be in a herd. Usually they graze in small, scattered bunches of from five or six to perhaps twenty head.

Each little group is led by one cow, very occasionally an old steer, and these little family parties have their own favourite ranges—perhaps one place for fly-time, one for noon siesta, and a different one for wet days. So that after a while you can pretty well depend on finding old Blue's family at the mouth of Saskatoon Coulee, or the broken-horned steer's bunch near the dry wash on Sheep Creek flats, and so on. This rule can't always be depended upon, because a bunch may suddenly leave a range for some reason—it may be for salt, it may be because their spring has dried up—but in course of time they will drift back.

Many of the small bunches headed by an old cow will represent her successive progeny over some years and probably some of their offspring. When the group gets too large to be a family, one of the elder daughters will probably split off with a following and form her own bunch. So old Blue's bunch consists of herself and her calf of the year, her yearling, her two-year-old, and her three-year-old daughter, the latter with her own new calf at foot.

The worst time to find cattle is in the hot days of July when the flies are out. If there is any brush or timber available the cattle will be there, and the way a hundred head can secrete themselves has to be seen to be believed. In the evening, however, they can be seen, when they are well scattered out for grazing; and also at the water-holes and springs, where the bunches come together to drink.

Every old cow knows her range, and after roundup, when the beef steers have been cut out for market, the cows drift back again and in only a few days you will probably find them at home. Hence the preconceived picture which so many people have of great herds of cattle and horses grazing on the plains is quite erroneous—unless, as I said before, they have been gathered by the cowboys.

Also the plains—at least in the cow country—must not be thought of as a vast level stretch, for the land is in fact rolling to hilly. It is so cut with shallow draws, as well as deep ravines and coulees, that although you can look straight across from the Cypress Hills to the Bear Paw Mountains in Montana without as much as a twig in the way, yet a rider can disappear from sight in five minutes.

Therefore, for either locating or rounding up cattle, knowledge both of their ways and of the country is indispensible in order not to do a lot of useless riding; and I might add that a good bump of location is also useful, for after riding circle you have to find your way back to camp, often after dark; and the camp may be invisible although quite close.

You might ask, what do the cowboys do? Well, that covers a lot of ground, because they do anything from mowing hay in summer to forking it out to the cattle in winter; from "riding fence," which means keeping the boundary fences in repair, to looking for strays missed on the roundup; from riding the water-holes and creeks to see how the supply is, to putting out salt when and where needed; from pulling bogged cows out of sinkholes to carrying the March-born calf of

48

a weak two-year-old in front of the saddle so that the mother will follow to the buildings for the hay she needs.

It goes without saying that in all this work horses are indispensible and are his constant companions, and he may change saddle horses two or three times a day in bad weather, or in early spring when the first calves are coming.

And that brings me to the annual calf crop, which is arranged to be dropped as nearly as possible just after new grass—in late April and early May if a late spring has not retarded growth. Here again don't jump to conclusions and think there are very few calves on the range because you see so many cows grazing around all alone. The calves aren't grazing yet, but just getting fat on their mothers' milk; and like young fawns they will be bedded down somewhere, invisible to the ordinary eye.

When a range cow is about to calve she leaves her companions and goes off alone. If she can find some willows, well and good; if not she seeks the quiet shelter of a draw or a small coulee, or the lee of a hill; and here she drops her calf, which arrives with a blat and a sneeze to open up its breathing apparatus. The mother immediately starts to lick it; and if it is strong and she is in good shape, it is soon wobbling on its clumsy legs and looking for breakfast. Coyotes often gather around and the mother has to be able to defend her precious young one.

The rider in charge of operations is quick to notice the absence of a cow and his job is to locate her and see that all is well. Many a time have I ridden over a knoll at dawn to see a cow standing over her new calf, her head lowered and horns looking very businesslike, while a coyote, or perhaps two or even three which have been looking on from the higher ground, slink quietly away. It is only very rarely that they do kill a calf. When the calf is strong on its legs the cows rejoins her bunch and introduces her offspring to its little fellows.

Thereafter the calves are generally bedded down all together in a sort of nursery, while the mothers graze as much as a mile distant—always, however, leaving one of their number as a nurserymaid. One of the most delightful sights imaginable is to come across such a group of calves—probably nowadays all of Hereford breeding, red with white faces and often "line backed" with white. If they are very young they don't move, but hug the ground, and you don't know they are there until your horse almost stumbles on one. And the way that not one, but possibly twenty or more calves, can lie hidden with no more cover than the prairie grass, and perhaps a scattering of sage-brush or rose briars, is simply uncanny.

If they are older and stronger on their pins they are as like as not to spring up and start stampeding around, bawling for their mothers. This brings the nurserymaid on the high lope; and it is as well to keep your distance, for in a very short time cows suddenly appear from every direction, all bawling and all looking like business.

The more the youngsters take to eating grass and the less depend-ent they are on milk, the more they follow the cows, until by August the calf nursery becomes only a noontime siesta ground. From all of which you will see that cattle have lost little of their wild habits over the years of domestication.

On in the summer the cattle are gathered and the calves are ear-marked and branded, and with December cold and snow they are weaned by being separated from their mothers and fed and watered in the calf corral, while the cows are hazed back to the range to put on a bit of flesh before the really hard winter of January. For a week or ten days the calves make night and day hideous with their incessant bawling—at least the racket would seem hideous to a lot of people, but to a cowman it is music of the sweetest. Odd cows, usually devoted young mothers, hang around the fences for several days as-sisting in the chorus, until they become so hoarse that one would think they suffered from laryngitis.

Range horses have similar habits and go in the same sort of bunches. And here I must take issue with those writers who give the impression that both wild horses and range horses go in great bands led by a stallion. True, there is in general a largish band; but except when rounded up or hazed, this is broken into small family groups keeping touch with each other. And while a stallion uses all his en-deavours to keep out other stallions, yet the real powers behind the throne are the wise old mares, who head the family groups, lead them to the water-holes, and take them to the best winter grazing; who knows the ways of riders and how to dodge them.

The old mares, wary of corral gates, wary of hissing ropes, wary of a rider silhouetted on the ridge, are able to enforce their will on the whole herd, including the stallion—whose place is not in front of the herd but behind, for he leaves the leading to the judgment of the mares and his role is to bring up the stragglers.

In looking for stray horses there are many things to know if you want to save yourself and your horse many miles of fruitless riding.

One thing to know is what range a lost horse came from before he was broken, because as a rule that is where you will find him. Another is to know if he has a special horse pal he is anxious to rejoin. And another thing to know is that in fly-time horses go to the hilltops in groups, and there they stand in pairs, head to tail, each with a muzzle on the other's rump to keep the flies from biting their sensitive lower lips. On a July day you can look through the heat haze at noon and see this. The same stretch of country may look completely deserted in the cool of early morning when the flies are dormant.

I've often located a bunch of horses by simply riding out in the morning and dismounting to let my horse graze, then leaning back against a rock to enjoy the sunshine while watching the hilltops. About eleven o'clock these begin to be tenanted, and pretty soon you know just how many head of horses range that particular piece of landscape, as they usually follow one another in single file, nodding their heads against the flies as they go, and are easily counted if not too far away.

In winter the range picture changes. The grass lands lie forsaken and desolate; but now as you approach a cattle ranch you will see life and movement, and cattle—plenty of them—contentedly munching the hay being forked out onto the ground from the big loads taken daily from the stacks. If it happens to be mild, without deep snow, you may see the winter field dotted thickly with cattle in full view of the house, grazing on the bleached grass which was allowed to grow unhindered last summer. And then your mental picture of a cattle ranch will have been realized.

Rounding up cattle on the western ranges is an activity quite often written of and shown on the screen nowadays. A legend has been built up about it as a great annual event, and an erroneous impression has been given of a sort of get-together of cowboys rather like a modern rodeo.

Actually it was a necessary operation and was work of the hardest kind. Discipline was strict, as it must be always wherever gangs of men work together. No work can be done properly by even two men unless one is boss; and just as a separator man on a threshing rig must be obeyed to the letter lest the machinery jam and time be lost, so the captain (to use a more southern term) of the roundup must be first among equals, able to make himself obeyed by orders given in what might, to others, sound like free-and-easy conversation, or even by a motion of the arm given out of earshot.

The cowboys rarely spoke of "riding on roundup;" they said riding with such-and-such a wagon. And while they might be in the saddle from 4:00 a.m. to 8 or 9 p.m., with a possible night shift of two hours thrown in, *their* activity was not called work. It was the wagon which was said to work the country.

In the days before the range was fenced, a large number of wagons worked the Canadian prairies from Wood Mountain in Saskatchewan to the Alberta foothills, and from the Red Deer River to the great Sandhills north of Maple Creek; besides which several wagons worked north from below the international boundary. One of these was the famous Circle outfit, so called from their brand. Occasionally wagons of different outfits met in the course of operations, but usually they kept clear of each other.

South of the Cypress Hills, the country was worked by the Cypress Hills pool wagon, and further east by the old 76—a famous brand still in existence. The first cattle to bear these figures were those of the Powder River Cattle Company of Northern Wyoming, founded by Moreton Frewen of Sussex, England, a friend of my father's. What was left of the herd after the disastrous winter killing of the late eighties, and the subsequent closing out of the company, was taken over by Sir Lester Keyes, who formed the Canadian 76 with headquarters at Crane Lake.

The North-West Mounted Police commonly used to send constables to ride with the wagons, sometimes for months. At times, however, the constables on detachment at such places as Ten Mile, Pendent d'Oreille, or Eastend, would visit the wagons when in the vicinity. Ten Mile detachment was on Battle Creek just south of Cypress Hills; Pendent d'Oreille a little north of the Sweet Grass Hills at the mouth of Earing Coulee. Eastend, as its name implies, was at the east end of Cypress Hills. It is now the site of a small town.

At the time of which I write the range was open and unfenced, and the ranchers got their grass free, or on very easy terms; and most outfits had what they call "line camps" strung along the limits of their range, from which "line riders" operated. By the way, when a rancher spoke of his "range," he meant the natural grazing area around his holdings. This old western usage came, like the first long-horned cattle and the wagons and cowboys themselves, from the Montana and Wyoming cattle country.

These hardy sun-bitten riders brought with them many things besides cattle and horses. They brought the Spanish words we use on the range; they brought southern-style cooking—heavy on syrup—and coffee; and they brought a tradition of loyalty to each other and the outfit.

Their fathers had left Texas after the War between the States, scorning to work like niggers with a hoe. They were horsemen, many of whom had been with Lee's ill-fated cavalry, and thus inured to hardship, hunger, thirst, and weary miles in the saddle. That explains the fourteen- or twenty-hour day so common when working with a wagon. The modern counterparts of these men are the drivers on the great overland truck routes.

These "Texans"—as they were mostly called, irrespective of their birthplace—had, moreover, the blood of adventurers, of *caballeros,* in their veins. As long as the open range lasted they could afford to ignore the "grangers"—the dirt farmers; but their enemy, the plow, had slowly but inevitably bitten deep into the southern grazing lands, so that the trend was ever west and north. And here in the Canadian West, the short-grass cowmen were making what we all thought was their last stand.

And yet it seems such a recent event that when a group of not-so-old-timers meet in Calgary or Maple Creek, the talk switches to scenes of romance and adventure which seem but yesterday.

Actually, the building of railroads and the coming of farmers did not mean the end of the range cattle business, only the inception of a more permanent and economical set-up. Much of the short-grass country was never taken up; and of the large amount that was, a great deal reverted to the ranchers in time—for the windswept places are old and will not be coerced. The great blizzards of the spring of 1905 which almost wrecked the cattlemen had their counterpart in those awful days of late March in 1938; but, in spite of heavy losses, the consequences of the latter storm were not nearly so serious, because the ranchers had learnt their lesson and hay was available.

But to return to the roundup. In those great open spaces the night camp was the only touch of civilization and group living for the men who rode with the wagon. Hence the wagon was symbolic of warmth, food, bed, clean shirts or socks, companionship, talk, and poker; and therefore it was the wagon which did the work. "I was with the 76 wagon," a man would tell you, as he would say, "I was living in Moose Jaw."

The boss of the outfit was not called just that, nor was he called the skipper or the super. To each trade belongs its own inviolable vocabulary and tradition, and the man who gave orders on the round-up was "the wagon boss."

One hears of the spring roundup and the fall roundup. In actual practice they were often one and the same thing as far as the big outfits were concerned. The wagon went out as soon as snow melted and the grass began to show green. It worked its allotted strip of country, camping at night at convenient water-holes, springs or creeks.

A necessary accompaniment to the twenty or fifty riders was their horses—anything up to half a dozen per cowboy, and each man's lot called his "string." This band of loose horses was called the "cavvy," and required two "wranglers," one to drive them with the wagon by day and one to herd them by night. Usually young fellows not fully experienced—like myself—did this work, which, although looked upon as menial, was still not without its responsibilities and its exciting moments.

On some outfits a chore man helped the cook with wood and water and tended the wagon teams, besides driving the "bed wagon" which carried the cowboys' "turkeys"—as they called their bedrolls, in which were wrapped their personal possessions such as tobacco—when the outfit was on the move. Commonly, however, these tasks had to be performed by the hoss wranglers.

When new mounts were needed, the cavvy would be run into a corral made by stretching ropes between the wagons—a mere bluff of a barrier, which, however, the wiry little cow ponies quite respected, for a rope was something they feared, with good reason.

But the wagon itself—the chuck-wagon—was the pride and joy of the outfit's (usually cranky) second in command, the roundup cook. His realm was sacred ground; and if you know how a bunch of hard-working young men can eat, you will see why he was as ready with a stick of wood or his fists as he was with his tongue. If he wasn't —well, the pie grabbers and coffee hounds would soon drag the whole outfit down to starvation rations.

"The boys," as the cook called them no matter what their ages got enough to eat and no more. Beans, pork, flapjacks and syrup, prunes, soda bread and coffee, topped off with a cigarette, goes good even three times a day, on the high prairies. The great treat was canned tomatoes.

The wagon itself was a heavy four-horse one, solidly built as it had need to be since it must go up hill and down dale, over dry washes, stony ridges, and muddy rivers, and would rarely see anything like a road.

Under its canvas top was all the cooking gear needed for the crew. Under the wagon was commonly slung a cowhide "cooney" into which dried brush or cow chips were chucked in event of a shortage of fuel. I have seen the bulky nests of sage twigs built by buzzards on the eroded cut banks pulled down and used to cook the men's food. A water barrel was part of the equipment, but only for emergency. At the back of the wagon was a tall built-in cupboard with deep shelves. This was the cook's pantry. Its door, hinged to the wagon bed, had a leg to prop it, parallel to the ground to form the cook's work table.

The fire sent up blue smoke at 4 a.m., and soon "Come and get it before I throw it out" would be heard; and, as if that were not invitation enough, the beating of an iron spoon against a skillet would arouse the heaviest sleeper.

The day riders would roll out from their beds on the prairie, throw their turkeys on the bed wagon, and line up for their tin plates of sowbelly with hotcakes and syrup, and their mugs of hot coffee. Then their mounts for the day were caught and saddled, and the wagon boss gave his orders—the direction of travel, etc.

The riders went off in twos to "make their circles." Each circle took in so much country, and the riders hazed all cattle within it towards camp. Sometimes they took a lunch in their saddle pockets, but more commonly their noon repast was a tight belt and a cigarette. In the fall, when the days got short, it sometimes wasn't too easy to find camp at night; and more than one cowboy has made a dry camp on the prairie.

After the day's gather, the work of branding began under the direction of the wagon boss. With no corrals to confine the herd, a number of the men had to hold the bunch by slowly riding round them. The rest of the cowboys were divided into groups. Two held the calf while one "ran the brand"—that is, put the registered mark on with the hot iron. Some of the men who ran the irons were real artists, and the speed with which they could put on a Running W, a Ladder, or a Jaydot was something to watch. It was customary to brand first all calves belonging to the outfit.

55

There had to be one man, usually old and experienced, to tend the branding fire and have the irons ready at the right heat. Nothing makes a crew madder than poorly heated irons. For each such crew was a "heeler," a mounted cowboy who would go into the heat and dust and noise of the herd to rope out the calves one at a time by the heels and drag the bawling and protesting infants up to the fire— sometimes with Mama in hot pursuit.

An additional job was to alter the young bulls. This operation, so fussed over by farmers with precautions by way of sterilizing and disinfecting, was and is performed on the range in a few moments. I still reckon to alter a calf in less than sixty seconds; and the fact that complications are almost unknown on the range is due to the dry, healthy air and ground.

After the wagon's cattle had been worked there were usually lots of others left—sometimes unbranded strays belonging to homesteaders or settlers. Here is where the Mounted Police came in, for I regret to say the average cowhand would have been quite prepared to put his outfit's brand on them, whereas the law required they be let go.

In an unfenced land and in spite of the line-riders' efforts to throw cattle from other outfits back from their line, it was inevitable that many cattle from different herds should be mixed. To take care of this, each outfit sent "reps" to the other wagons.

You will hear a man say, "I was with the Spencer wagon repping for the 76," and that means he was riding with the wagon down on the Milk River ridge, representing the 76 brand far from its own headquarters at Crane Lake. His job was to work like any other cowboy under the wagon boss; and when the outfit's calves had been branded, he and the other reps, each in turn, would be told to start working the cattle of whatever brands they represented. (The calves stayed close to their mothers, and thus could be identified by the brands on the latter.)

When all the cattle had been worked they were turned loose, ownership established now, for each calf carried its mother's brand; and they speedily drifted off to their accustomed haunts, while the wagon went on to repeat the process further on.

That was spring, or calf, roundup; but as I said, with a large range to cover, a wagon sometimes stayed out all summer and on into fall, so that their later activities consisted of what was called

fall roundup, the purpose of which was to gather the marketable beef steers. The procedure was the same, except that after each day's work the beef were cut out from the herd by mounted cowboys, and made into a separate herd called the "beef cut." After the unmarketable and breeding stock was turned loose, this beef herd was kept with the wagon, which necessitated men being told off for herd duty by day as well as by night.

Usually everyone did a two-hour spell of night herd, or "guard" as it was sometimes called; and the stories one reads of stampedes and terrible nights with cattle may not all be true, but all could be; for a bunch of big steers are twice as "spooky" as a mixed bunch, and one old "mossy horn" steer getting to its feet on the bed ground with a grunt and a blow would often be enough to start something.

That is why the night herder sang. It wasn't for the music's sake, and melody as such has no power to soothe the savage steer. Talking to oneself or one's horse would have served the same purpose; but among a bunch of men, to talk to oneself was to run the risk of being called a sheepherder—a deadly insult. The reason behind the singing was to let the herd know where you were, and that you weren't a lobo or a dust devil; and it was also to let your opposite number know the same. Nights can be dark on the prairie.

There were no lovesick crooning cowboys in those days; or if the odd one did have dreams of pretty Sally at Maple Creek, he kept them to himself.

With luck the work was finished by the time snow flew, and the wagons pulled for home and the boys for Maple Creek, Medicine Hat, or "Haver" across the line, with the accumulation of forty a month burning a hole in their pockets. Most of the boys heading south would be reps from the American outfits, taking their cut with them.

Talking about wagons, I must, at the risk of offending old-time cowmen, mention the men who are the backbone of the range sheep industry—the sheepherders, as we call the Scottish, Mexican, or Basco (Basque) shepherds.

They too are men of the wagon; but even more so than the cowboys, for a whole wagon is the home of one, or at most two, sheepherders; and in this covered wagon, reminiscent of a gypsy caravan, they cook, eat, rest, and sleep. There is no pantry at the back, but let-down steps; there is a snug stove in the corner, a bunk, shelves, and perhaps even a rug on the floor. Usually there are no horses to look after, because they do not use saddle horses, and moving the wagon is done by a "camp tender" from the home ranch who comes, perhaps weekly, by team, to bring grub and mail and to move camp.

Alone on the sere high prairie, the brittle grass and redolent sage beneath his feet, the limitless horizon before his eyes, the blue of space above his battered hat, the sheepherder stands in the annals of the West—today as yesterday, the same quiet, patient, painstaking man as on the desert of Sinai, the pampas of old Spain, or the downs of England.

His crook is his badge of office, his dogs his loyal servants, his band of wooly charges his whole purpose. A thousand sheep is called a "band"—not a flock; that would be farmer parlance.

Semper fidelis. The old motto might well fit the lean, suntanned men of the rowel and lariat, or the patient, brave, and lonely men of the crook. In a big world of sky and prairie, where winds blow harsh, who could be blamed too much if he slipped away and left the dust of the wagon or the solitariness of the bleating band? And yet—whoever did?

The range was being torn by the plow, the spools of barbed wire were being stretched with a metallic screech, by the time I was experienced enough to be promoted from herding the cavvy to the full glory of riding a circle.

The day of the general roundup was over, and thereafter only the larger lease areas were worked by wagon, and a week or two sufficed to get the job done.

PACK TRAILS

CHAPTER SIX

The Chilcotin

I HAD met Frank on the boat coming back from overseas, and his description of Chilko Lake and the Chilcotin, in the interior of British Columbia, had fired me with the desire to see that country. So here I was, having come up the Cariboo Road with horses I had bought at the Indian rancherie at Clinton.

All the way up The Road, as it is called, I kept thinking that now I knew what this country looked like; but presently it would change again, and I decided I would have to see a whole lot of it before I would be able really to grasp its distinctive features.

Here are open rugged hills and buttes which remind one of the Cypress Hills, for the Chilcotin too is in the dry belt. Next we see great forests of evergreens broken by long-grass muskegs, just like parts of northern Manitoba, except for being tipped on edge instead of lying flat. Then we come to a series of grass benches cut by coulees (called gulches in this province), which look like the hillsides of Saskatchewan's Qu'Appelle Valley on a broader and larger scale. The river flats, overgrown with sage and cactus, might be those at Medicine Hat; and the dense, rolling poplar woods remind one of the Eagle Hills near Battleford.

But the mountains are British Columbia's own—that jagged, ice-capped range which is the Cascades. They dominate the country, making it like—like the Chilcotin and nothing else.

True, one catches only occasional glimpses of the peaks from the road, but one *feels* them—feels that all these gullies and ravines and rugged hills are but an introduction to those high peaks and inaccessible alpine meadows.

Perhaps it is the wind that makes one feel them—that wind laden with the odour of evergreens and having the sharpness of ice in it. Or perhaps it is the rivers, for in place of the placid and steady flow of the prairie rivers, these—the Chilcotin and its tributaries the Chilko, the Taseko, and the Chilankoh—hurry toward the Fraser impatiently, swirling around sharp bends, fretting away solid rock, and foaming over the gravel bars with a steady roar.

From the 150 Mile House on the Cariboo Road to Alexis Creek, whence the narrow pack trails branch off to Chilko Lake and the Tatlayoko Country, is two or three days' travel by pack and saddle. The route is a winding wagon road, which traverses the Riske Creek prairie, and then more or less parallels the Chilcotin River. This is cattle country, and the log houses and roomy corrals of the ranchers are mostly located along the river flats, which are irrigated for their hay crops. The patches of green timothy and clover are in rich contrast to the burnt yellow hills which rise in a series of high benches, dotted with bunch grass.

At the highest bench begins the general level of the country— for rugged as it is, this interior plateau does have a general level, rolling away east to the Cariboo country and westward to lap the feet of the mountains.

It appears to be all timbered "stick country," covered with aspen, poplar, and lodgepole pine, with here and there fairly open stands of Douglas fir; but on riding over it you can see its value as summer range. There are numerous open, grassy hills, and dozens of old beaver meadows, which, with the rich grass and pea vines of the more open timber stretches, make very good grazing.

By pushing the cattle up over the rimrock—as they call the crest of the hills—to scatter out for the summer, the ranchers are able to conserve the bunch-grass hillsides nearer home for their winter range.

The bunch grass is quite tall and grows in separate bunches interspersed with grey wormwood, as our familiar pasture sage is called here. It cures in the fall in the same manner as the grass of the prairie ranges, making a strong feed on which a horse will travel all day without grain. Horses can winter out in bands roaming the more open country and pawing through snow when necessary, just as they do in the cow country of the plains. This "winter rustling," as they call it on the prairies, becomes "bunch-grassing it" in the Chilcotin.

At the Chilko River crossing I met a party of Chilcotin Indians camped among the willows, who told me in broken English and

Chinook that the river was too high to cross, and like them I should have to wait till the flood went down. The high water was the result of the extremely hot weather, which was thawing the snow and ice on the peaks to the west.

So I made camp, hobbling my saddle-horse, and leaving the pack-horse free till night, when I put him on picket. My bedding and grub were soon unpacked and all made snug, with coffee boiling on the red coals and sending its aromatic odour to mingle with the scent of pine and melting snow.

Coffee was introduced into the West by the Texans and other cattlemen from the States; and no better brew can be had than that which the cowboy makes squatting over a fire of cow chips or dry twigs. Later, in the North, I was to find coffee almost unknown; for long ago the Hudson's Bay Company had introduced tea to the Crees and Salteaux, and that beverage is universal in the Northland.

Canada jays soon sought out my camp and swept downward with their silent flight to perch on the lower limbs of the scattered firs on the look-out for tidbits. In the Interior they are often called "camp robbers," in contrast to the universal name of "whiskey jack" which they enjoy around Hudson Bay, and which is a corruption of the Cree "weeskee-poos." Two nutcrackers also came in view, bent on the same errand. These were the first of that species I had seen, and I was interested to note the extreme wariness of these grey-and-white birds, with their shiny black wings and tails, and long bills.

From the Indian camp came the sound of talking and laughing until their fire went out, and all was quiet except for the roaring of the Chilko River.

Crossing mountain rivers looks more dangerous than it is. When the flood subsided, the water was little more than knee high; but so swiftly did it flow over the gravel bar at the ford, and so white with froth was it, that it certainly made one uneasy, especially as it was a quarter of a mile across.

Mine were mountain horses, however; and having once put their muzzles down to gauge the depth and swiftness of the river and the quality of the footing, they stepped in willingly enough and made for the further shore.

I got used to it afterwards, but that first time I didn't like the feeling of moving sideways as if the current had one in its grasp; but it was only the foaming water swirling past that gave that impression,

and by looking at the bank on the other side, I soon restored my proper sense of balance. Of course, these rivers can be dangerous and accidents do happen; poor Frank himself finally met his death by drowning while crossing this same river a few years later.

In winter, when high ice forms on either shore, it is quite a trick to get one's horse off it and into the water—and more of a trick to pull and coax him out on the other side. Unlike the prairie rivers, these streams rarely freeze completely over in winter.

A common trick of the Chilcotin Indians is to cut down a few young, green spruce or pine trees somewhere close to these fords, during their summer trips. Then after a winter crossing which leaves their legs encased in ice, they have only to set a match to one of these trees, now dry and red-needled, and presto! there is a hot fire in a minute to dry them off.

The blazed trail wound on through lodgepole pine which had been burnt over some years before. The black, fallen trunks criss-crossed in all directions, impeding the progress of the horses as they stepped over them. Many pack horses had done this in the past years, so that the narrow trail was worn into deep holes where they had stepped between the logs. Through this tangle of burnt trees sturdy second-growth pine, about four feet high already, was pushing upward in hundreds.

This was an Indian hunting trail which led to Chilko Lake and around the shoulder of Tenas Mountain to the Nemiah Valley, and therefore an important route to them; but unless a fallen log was breast high, they did not bother to chop it out—and not even then if they could find a way around the end.

I stopped to shoot a young grouse for supper, and profiting by the teaching of an old plains half-breed in my prairie days, tied it in front of the saddle by winding the leather tie-strings around the base of a wing. Birds carried like this are safe all day—walk, trot, or gallop—and never annoy one by banging about. The natural crook of the bird's wing and the stiff flight feathers prevent the thong from slipping, as usually happens if a bird is tied on by the feet. To tie by the head may mean only a head at camp that night, for the body wrenches from the neck fairly easily.

The bird I shot was a lovely one, slightly different from the spruce grouse of the Saskatchewan woods. I got to know this variety as Franklin's grouse, with the tail darker and narrowly tipped with dingy white rather than buff.

On this trail I heard for the first time the cry of the loon, a cry I was to hear many times both night and day in northern Saskatchewan and Manitoba.

We finally left the pine ridge and debouched into the valley of Tsuniath Lake, a long, narrow body of water, almost an arm, extending easterly from the much larger Chilko Lake, from which it is separated by a narrow neck of land with a short connecting creek.

After the dreary burnt country, the hay flats and bunch-grass hillsides of the valley were a welcome relief; and the horses broke into a smart trot which soon brought Frank's cabin into view. It was built mountain style—that is, with the door at one end, over which the roof of poles and sod, fuzzy with weeds and grass which had seeded themselves thereon, projected some six feet and formed a porch.

On the door was a roughly pencilled note to tell me that Frank was away, and that I was to help myself to grub until he came back.

From the cabin door, which faced the lake, one could look down its length at the icicle-like peaks of the Cascades, in whose very shadows we appeared to be. At times one thought one could hear the murmur of the Pacific beyond that almost impassable wall. It was impassable at all but one point; and that point, Waddington Pass, was so beswept by gales and blinding storms in summer, and so completely choked with snow in winter, as to have been traversed but rarely since the days when the wild coast Indians were wont to make their raids into the hunting grounds of the Chilcotins.

Partly because of the storms and cold and snow, but partly also because of those dim memories, the Indians of Chilko Lake never penetrate that far; to them it is a *cultus* place—a bad place.

At the far foot of the pass lies what is still called Waddington Harbour, at the narrow end of a fjord-like inlet that winds inland from the sea to bring salt water within sixty miles of Chilko Lake. It is a harbour only in name, and proved no safe anchorage for the little vessel that disembarked its crew there many years ago for rest and fresh water. They perished almost to a man in the massacre which followed—a crime committed by the warlike and murderous Salt Water Siwashes.

In all that great opposite slope of spruce and pine, gorges and high basins, lived only one man—and a white man at that, the old French-Canadian trapper, Alex Ducharme.

The mountains west of Chilko Lake are marten country; and as marten is one of the really fine furs and always in demand, the animal is worth a good deal of time and trouble to trap. Its chief food consists of squirrels; and these steep slopes, heavily timbered with evergreens, form a natural breeding-ground for those small rodents.

In one of the higher basins in the mountains directly west of Chilko Lake was the cabin of Alex Ducharme, a hermit who lived almost entirely on the meat of wild goats, and to boot, made his winter supply of candles from their tallow.

Ducharme had one special *bête noire*—gold prospectors, or in fact anyone interested in minerals. There was colour to be found in all the little creeks on his trap line, and also a fine outcrop of copper ore; but the old man never spoke of it, and scared away every prospector —and they were few and far between—who questioned him. He had it figured out that if anybody got really interested in that vein of copper, some company would eventually come in with machinery and build a road; and that would be the end of his trap line.

Ducharme was an expert trapper and an able woodsman, and he made very good catches. He was never troubled by Indians; as I have said, they kept out of the mountains, which they feared not only for superstitious reasons but as the supposed habitation of evil men, the Ankiti Siwashes.

One day in the beginning of March I saw a black dot coming across Chilko Lake and heading for the Tsuniath Narrows and the cabin. It had been mild for weeks, and now the sun was as hot as in spring.

About noon the dot was close enough for me to see that it was Ducharme. As I had not seen a white man since Christmas, I was glad to welcome him at the lake shore. He was bearded and filthy after a winter alone in the mountains, and was pulling a toboggan piled high with bales of fur and rather smelly goat meat.

"By gar," he greeted me, "you new fellow stop with François, eh?" I told him yes, and added that I was alone for the winter. "By gar," he went on, "pretty soon I t'ink she going be springtime, huh? I'm pretty scare for hice she going out maybe; so I mak queek trip ovair de lac —not stop for camp."

It was nearly twenty miles across Chilko Lake, and he lived another ten beyond that. It was over forty miles more to the post at Redstone; so what he was doing on the trail in March, with another month of the trapping season left, mystified me. As a rule these old trappers didn't leave their lines between November and April. So I asked him why he was going out.

"Sure I just tol' you why," he said. "Pretty soon hice she go out." I asked him what date he thought it was. "I guess she pretty near middle of Hapril, eh? Maybe not quite"—squinting at the sun—"sometam I lose track, seems lak."

And when I told him it was only the beginning of March, he hardly believed me until I showed him my calendar with the days crossed off. Then his chagrin was both comical and tragic. *"Sapri—* I'm t'inkin' on all dose marten I'm leave in de hills," he grumbled; but finally he decided to call it a season.

Next day I helped him to catch his pack-ponies, which had wintered in Frank's meadow, and he pushed on down the trail, having, with the air of a grandee, made me a present of the odoriferous goat meat.

I realized that the old man was getting "bushed," as they say, and therefore was not surprised that the following winter brought a tragedy to Chilko Lake.

68

For some years Ducharme had felt that he was getting too old to trap alone; and that spring after selling his furs he made a trip to Vancouver, where he met a strapping young Swede, to whom he proposed a partnership. They went in together the next winter and took turns on the line and with the cooking.

During their conversations in the city the Swede had made no mention of being interested in anything but trapping; but before long he started a little quiet prospecting on his own, and brought several samples of ore to the cabin. This led to a row, and Ducharme told his partner bitterly that if he had known that he was a prospector as well as a trapper, he would have made no deal with him.

The Swede thought little of it, not knowing how vicious a bee the old man had in his bonnet when it came to prospectors. He was completely surprised, on returning one bitterly cold night from the exhausting toil of twenty miles on the trap line, to find that Ducharme, who had evidently been brooding about things, was waiting for him in the open cabin door with a levelled 30.30.

The Swede asked what was the big idea, and Ducharme told him to hike down the trail and keep on hiking. The young man argued that it was thirty-five below, his clothes were full of snow, and he couldn't travel without a change of clothes, some grub, and a blanket or two. But Ducharme was adamant. He locked himself in and kept watch with the rifle. Every time the Swede approached he was met with a rifle shot.

He made a fire in the bush, and tried to snare rabbits; but the rabbit plague was on, and the one thin animal he got was so diseased that he dared not attempt to eat it. After two days in which all parley failed, the young man was in a very exhausted condition. He had no choice but to shoot Ducharme in order to obtain food and shelter. The shot was fatal.

After a good feed and a rest the young Swede was sufficiently recovered to wrap the old man's body in a tarpaulin and lodge it up a tall tree, from which he then cut off the lower branches in order that wild animals might not disturb the corpse. Then, adjusting his heavy packsack to his shoulders, he tramped down to the settlements to give himself up to the police. If I remember rightly, he was acquitted.

Speaking to me of this tragedy some years later, he said: "I know where the gold is, and that copper vein is one of the biggest I have ever seen; but you know, life is more precious than gold. Yust for that one man had to be killed and one man had to be the killer, so I want to forget all about it.

Frank's reaction to the affair was: "Well, that's what comes of living off goats."

CHAPTER SEVEN

Siwashes

The Chilcotin Indians are of Athapaskan stock, allied to the Carrier Indians of northern British Columbia and the Beavers, Dogribs and Chipwyans of the more easterly woodlands. Although there are general points of similarity between all Canadian Indians, the Athapaskan group have little in common so far as language is concerned with the Blackfeet and Dakotas of the plains, or the large Algonquin-Cree-Chippewa family north and west of the Great Lakes. The great point of similarity, of course, is the fact that they live by hunting.

Although they own small reserves—which they call rancheries—most of them prefer a nomadic life, roaming the rugged wilderness between Gang Ranch and the Tatlayoko Lake, hunting and fishing as the spirit and the game supply move them.

They take a good deal of fur, which they trade at the various posts for the flour, baking-powder, tea, sugar, and tobacco which they require, as well as for fancy saddles and chaps, and bright prints for their womenfolk.

Yet they can hardly be called trappers in the Hudson Bay meaning of the term, because they rarely run a proper line of traps and snares, but prefer to hunt on horseback with a rifle in the crook of the arm and a few odd dogs—mean-tempered and of uncertain breed. Most of the lynx, cougar, fox and wolf they sell are taken with a bullet in this way.

This is not a deep-snow country—except in the higher peaks, which the Indians shun—and what snow does fall usually stays for but a few days in the open before being wiped out by the chinook wind, or else blown into the gullies if it stays cold. The bush holds the snow better, but in any case its depth is rarely such as to impede horses from travelling and grazing out.

Therefore, snowshoes are known only as a strange accoutrement of the "Stick Indians," who inhabit the area north from the Blackwater basin, and with whom the Chilcotins sometimes come in contact. The Chilcotins themselves always travel mounted, usually leading one or more pack horses loaded with gear—which may include the toddlers of the family.

They own many ponies, hardy little beasts akin to the wild ones which range the mountain meadows, and are quite unconcerned about how they use them. They are never stabled, but "bunch grass it" summer and winter.

The Chilcotins do not compare in horsemanship, however, with the plains Indians—especially the Blackfeet, who have used horses a good deal longer. As the wild Spanish horses of Coronado's time were made use of by the Comanches and the Pawnees, they speedily extended their range northward as the Gros Ventres and the Crows obtained them by capture and trade; and these tribes in turn supplied the Blackfeet.

But the mountain cayuses came in from the broken plateau country west of the Rockies by way of the Nez Percé and Flathead Indians, and were commonly called Oregon horses. So it took them many years to cross the jagged mountain ranges and establish themselves in the British Columbia interior.

Of course the wild horses constantly augmented their ranks by harbouring renegade ranch stock, for horses love to go wild, and in a great unfenced country like the Chilcotin ranchers could not always prevent this.

I remember one old mare that used to run with a small band of cayuses on Tenas Mountain, who still had part of a hobble dangling from her foreleg; but make no mistake—she was as wild and wary as any mustang, and leaped through the deadfall as surely.

The language of these Indians among themselves is Chilcotin, which sounds like a collection of guttural clicks, like all the Athapaskan tongues; and indeed a Chilcotin from west of the Fraser River can converse quite freely with a Chipwyan from north-east Saskatchewan.

To whites they speak in broken English and Chinook—the latter being a sort of trade language composed of various Indian, English, and corrupted French words, based on the language of the Chinook Indians of the Oregon country. It is the *lingua franca* of most of the inter-mountain region from Oregon to Alaska.

The word "Siwash" itself is Chinook, and is a corruption of the French *sauvages,* which was the word always used by the early French explorers and *coureur de bois* when speaking of Indians. It was, I believe, originally used to denote the coast Indians only, who are a fish-eating, salt-water folk, living in villages, and quite different in feature and habits from the nomadic Chilcotin horsemen. However, most ranchers of the interior loosely refer to all Indians as Siwashes. In the one matter of being horsemen, they are somewhat like the plains Indians, with whom they have come in contact through the Shuswaps; but whereas both sexes among the Blackfeet and Stoneys (Dakotas) customarily wear their hair long and in two careful plaits, the male Siwashes bob theirs off around the ear in an untidy way, and only the younger women braid theirs.

The Cree youngsters, too, wear their little plaits; but the rather dirty, though quite lovable, Chilcotin children allow their hair to grow as it wishes. This gives them a wild look when it is flying in the

R·D·S·

wind, and a horribly sullen expression when it hangs over their eyes as they crouch around the camp fire.

The Chilcotins live either in untidy camps on the trail—no neat tipis for them—or, more rarely, in semi-permanence in small log huts with dirt floors. In the old days, they say, they lived underground in community dwellings called *kikiliholes*—a type of which has been in use in quite recent times among their relatives the Carriers. These were large circular dugouts with a roof of poles covered with brush and earth, and an entrance hole in the middle with a ladder leading to it. This hole served also to let out the smoke of the cooking fires.

Here, apparently, several families denned in for the winter. The remains of some of these old dugouts are still to be seen. Probably they were given up about the middle of the last century, when the spread of horses into these mountains permitted the Indian to be more nomadic and independent as to his movements.

The Chilcotins are inveterate gamblers. I remember one, who had been baptized Charlie Francis by the French missionary from down the road—for most of these people are nominal Christians—who though nothing of literally losing his shirt.

He rode by the cabin one day, complete with bright shirt and decorated chaps, topped off by one of the stiff-brimmed stetsons so beloved by the older plains Indians and still worn, at the time of which I write, in the mountains. He rode a splendid little roan horse equipped with a fine new stock saddle.

He stopped and visited for a while, and drinking sweet tea, told me he was on his way to a potlatch or "give-away dance" at Nemiah Valley. "Plenty good time stop. Plenty dances, plenty song, plenty play *la hille*."

La hille is the "stick game," rather like *see-sip wuk* or "game of the ducks" of the Ojibways. It is a sort of hunt-the-slipper game, but there are many slippers and the guesser has to locate them all. It is played with tremendous enthusiasm, the players sitting in a circle and chanting the *la hille* song long into the night.

"Mebbeso," Charlie went on, "helo chikamun stop I come back," meaning that he might return broke. And so it proved.

About a week later he came back, a somewhat sorry figure—bareheaded, stripped of his gaudy shirt and his fringed chaps, and bestriding a boney old mare without benefit of saddle.

"Hi-ya tillicum," he greeted me. "You plenty muck-a-muck stop?

74

Me hyu sick tum-tum. That place"—indicating the Nemiah Valley with a wave of his hand—"plenty no good, plenty cultus Siwash. Me helo hat stop—helo saddle stop—helo chikamun stop."

"Never mind, Charlie," I said, "I'll feed you this time and p'raps you'll win it all back next time."

"Sure," he grinned, quite happy at the thought of good grub, "me plenty everyt'ing stop *next time*."

In the summer many of these Indians go to work temporarily for the white ranchers down-river, especially for hay-making. In spite of the comparatively mild winters, some hay is required by the stock, and even Frank, who was just making a start with about thirty cows, had ingeniously packed in a mower and a hayrake on pony-back—in pieces, of course—to be reassembled at Tsuniath Valley.

One Indian called Jack Loola—or more commonly Crazy Jack—engaged to rake Frank's hay while I mowed. First thing in the morning I carefully showed him how to oil and grease the machine and told him to repeat the process several times a day. "Me savvy," he said, so I left him to it. To see that Indian trot over the hay field and swing his team around as he bunched the windrows was a sight only to be compared with a Roman chariot race.

At noon I yelled to him to unhitch for dinner. On my way in I stopped to look at the hayrake. If ever anything needed greasing, that did. "Jack," I said, "you haven't done what I told you. See, you've got to keep those wheels greased so," and I did it myself. Jack looked solemn, very solemn. "*Now* me savvy," he said.

Jack used to regale me with weird stories of the Antkiti Siwashes, the Indian giants who lived in bygone days at Chilko Lake and who, the Indians thought, still turned up unexpectedly.

"One tam," Jack told me, "me see um that Ankiti Siwash—my hyu scare—all he dlaid hyu (extremely) tall—he helo shirt his back; he helo mocassin his feet; helo hat his head stop—just plenty hair like bush. Me no savvy see-um that fellow before—me hyu cumtux (guess) him Ankiti Siwash! Me go way that place all same cultus coulee."

These Indians always seemed to be travelling "cultus coulee," which means moving about with no set destination, and stopping wherever there is good hunting or fishing. Contrariwise, to "go klatawa" is to go visiting at some special place—perhaps one of the rancheries—and they like to travel straight through, not even stopping to camp unless forced to. They commonly ride at a fairly easy jog for the first twenty or thirty miles, but always plan to fairly dash into the camp or post they are visiting.

On my way down to Alexis Creek one Christmastime I was caught up with by about forty Chilcotins with a long string of pack-ponies. They came along singing away as they do in a wailing minor. They invited me to travel with them. At Bidwell Creek the leader—they always travel single file, pack-horses driven loose in twos or threes between riders—suddenly swung off into the bush, which was fairly open pine with a good deal of five-foot second growth.

Charlie, the man just ahead of me, told me over his shoulder that they were on their way to a Christmas potlatch at the Anahim rancherie, and they had made a bet to get there from Eagle Lake in one day. So they were going to go like hell and "cut country."

On we went, over rugged uplands and across deep ravines where they slid down on their ponies and hit the cold creeks with a splash that almost hid each rider before his pony scrambled up the opposite bank. They laughed at me for dismounting and letting my horse go ahead, loose, up the steep long banks of the ravines. A good rider who considers his horse always does this, grabbing the animal's tail with one hand. The horse pulls one up with far less exertion than if it had to pack a rider, and there is practically no effort for the man, who feels himself quite comfortably lifted to the top.

Since the Indians couldn't possibly understand a white man's regard for his mount, I never tried to explain and simply let them think —as they did—that I was frightened of the steepness.

Every now and then one of them would lean from the saddle to break off the top of a young pine. In this way the trail was marked, in case snow covered their tracks, for anyone who by chance might get left behind. At the end of roughly each hour, the leading Indian would drop to the rear and the one behind him take his place as trail maker. Great were the chaffing comparisons between the ability of these different men to follow the easiest course consistent with maintaining the general south-easterly direction.

We had come rather slowly through a bad *brulé*, when the Indian in the lead stopped and the whole cavalcade halted abruptly. With much laughter from the men and giggling from the women, they delved into the various packs, producing coloured silk scarves, fancy beaded gloves and other finery, with which they adorned themselves gaily. I judged we must be getting close to the main road and they were preparing to meet "company." Then came a great adjusting of packs, as the sweating horses nuzzled around in the dry timber-grass. Lash ropes were tightened till the pack animals grunted, and saddles cinched to the last quarter inch.

Then Charlie turned to me. *"Now* we ride," he said. And we certainly did—hell for leather, over interlaced logs where a fall meant a horse snagged deep in the belly, down half-icy hillsides where the ponies' unshod hooves slid straight from top to bottom—and how they kept their balance only Pegasus knows.

My conjecture was correct. After about ten miles of this, we suddenly came out to the pack trail on the east side of the Chilcotin River. The Indians turned south to cross at the nearby Anahim rancherie, while I turned north for Alexis Creek.

That is klatawa.

Cultus coulee, on the other hand, means that if you see a deer track, you're free to leave the trail and follow it. Wonderful trackers, the Chilcotins scan the trail and surrounding ground always. Where you or I might see nothing, the Indian will suddenly see the print of a deer—perhaps on dry or gravelly ground. "Mowitch," he will grunt and, pulling his rifle out of its scabbard, whirl his pony and follow that track on the dead lope. And he usually gets the deer.

Jack Loola once visited me travelling cultus coulee. His wife had died a couple of years before and he hardly every stayed very long in one place, and of necessity had to take his children with him. About three days before he landed up I had seen a fresh lynx track on Tullin Mountain. Jack at once asked my permission to leave his brood in my care, and this granted, he whistled to his dogs and was off.

Nearly a week later—a week in which the little varmints had made sad inroads into my grubstake—he returned. He had shot the lynx after three days' tracking. His dogs treed it and his rifle brought it down. He had only a little bannock and tea to live on during the hunt, but after the kill he broiled the lynx meat over his camp fire—a very good meat he said it was, "like labbit"—and then had a long sleep.

That is their trade. The Chilcotin Indians are easy-going, rather lazy, rather dirty creatures. But as trackers they are unexcelled, and as hunters they are keen and untiring. It is to be hoped that they may long continue to enjoy in peace the rugged foothills of the Cascade range.

CHAPTER EIGHT

Crazy Jack

FRANK WAS away down the road to Ashcroft and I was alone, as I would be most of the winter. One night, soon after going to bed, I heard a shout "Hi-yi hi-yi"—the common greeting with which to approach a camp. Presently the man thumped at the door and then came in, pulling long icicles from that part of his scarf which enveloped his lower face. It was Jack Loola.

"Hi Jack," I called from the bunk, "what's up?" He knelt down by the little sheet-iron camp stove, and blew the sparks to life before he answered, "Me hyu sick tum-tum. My papoose going mamaloosh I t'ink. All same he girl fell in fire. All his back he burn. Gimebye you come mebbseo? Mebbeso savvy fix-um?"

"When did this happen, Jack?" I asked, pulling my pants on. He waved to the south. "All same Taseko Lake my camp stop," he said. "Are your wife and kids there?" I asked, forgetting that he was a widower. "Goman [woman] he long time mamaloosh. All same t'ree boy, two girl stop me. Me fix 'em all time. Goman he mamaloosh."

"O.K., Jack," I said, "we'll have some tea and bannock, and I'll saddle up and come with you and see what I can do."

So we fed and hit the trail. I took some tea, sugar, and flour, well knowing the meagerness of Indian larders. Also some carbolic ointment. But what I relied on most was a large jar of "Denver Mud" (Antiphlogistine) and several old but clean white shirts.

It was twenty-five miles to Taseko Lake, a wild and almost unknown territory, to reach which we had to take the pack trail over the hogsback of Tenas Mountain, where the wind blew our horses' manes and tails at right angles. The cold was intense, but the snow was not very deep. Jack led—a muffled figure, dim and indistinct in the starlight as he wound his way between the dark pines.

Half-way there we stopped and built a fire, drank hot tea, and had a smoke, while Jack told me more of the situation. Deer were scarce and wild in the Choelquoit Lake area, where he usually lived; so he had taken his family with him on a hunting trip in the Taseko bottomlands, camping at the edge of the lake. He got one deer and left the children to take care of the hide and meat, while he went to follow another fresh track he had seen.

When he got back with a second deer, he found that his eldest girl, age twelve, was badly burned. The term papoose is commonly used among the natives to denote children of almost any age, but still I had expected a much younger patient.

Jack went on to explain that the child had tried to rescue the deer hide, which had fallen into the camp fire. She had hung it over the fire to melt off the fat as a treat—rather like a white kiddie licking a spoon. It was naughty to risk damage to a deer hide, because the Indians depend upon these for tanning into moccasin leather.

Somehow she had tripped and fallen into the fire, which was much too large—no doubt the children had felt the eeriness of the dark forest during their father's absence and had replenished the blaze too rapidly. As she attempted to get up, her foot apparently caught under a kettle stick, so that she lay there long enough to burn her back badly.

The stars had dimmed and grey dawn was breaking in the east when we got to the camp. Wild-looking dogs raised their hackles and barked as we approached the brush shelter, in front of which the ashes of last night's fire still sent up a faint blue wisp of smoke. With the barking the shelter came to life, and out popped four heads of tangled black hair from which eight big black eyes stared.

Jack spoke in Chilcotin, and I suppose he told them not to be frightened of the white man. At all events they came shyly forth, three smallish boys and a very small girl, all in dirty nondescript garb and worn moccasins, evidently their attire by night as well as by day.

Within lay the injured child, among a collection of shabby blankets and rabbin-skin robes. She lay on her stomach, and as I knelt down to investigate, she shrank back into her tangled hair and stared with wild frightened eyes, I patted her arm and Jack spoke again, and she lay still.

Stripping off the dirty blankets, I exposed the worst burn I have ever seen. From between the shoulders right down to the base of her spine she was one horrible crusted mass, in which bits of her shabby print dress were embedded.

I covered her again, and melted snow until all the various pots and kettles in camp were full of warm water. Slowly and very carefully I softened up the crust enough to remove the half-burned bits of cloth, and then washed her as much as I could without moving her. Jack made no attempt to help—thank goodness, for his dirty fingers might have increased the danger.

She was a splendid little patient and neither moved nor moaned, although my attentions must have been torture—so much so that I thought she might have fainted, and stooped in concern to see her face; but her eyes were wide open.

The washing complete, it was only a matter of minutes to plaster her back thickly with the healing clay, which would exclude all air and dirt, and then cover it with a clean shirt bound on with strips torn from another. The ointment I did not use at all.

Then we all had sweet hot tea without milk—that panacea for all troubles to the Indian—flavoured strongly with spruce from the needles picked up with the snow for melting. Jack Loola's injured papoose drank with the rest.

I gave him instructions simply to leave everything as it was, and not move her for a week—and above all not to try to pry under the bandages—and then I would try to come and see her again. Not caring to share the Indians' verminous bedding, and having brought none of my own, I then started for home.

About a week later—in milder weather, for the chinook was at last blowing—I went to see my patient. The healing was almost perfect, but I repeated the process and told Jack to let the girl take the bandages off herself in another week, and then she should be all right.

Many weeks later, in muskrat time, Jack Loola again called at the cabin with his ragged family.

"You good mans, Shomons," he said, shaking hands. "Gimebye you mamaloosh [die]. You go Saggali Tyee [God]. Saggali Tyee say, 'You good mans. You savvy fix-um lil papoose stop Jack Loola.'"

And Jack Loola's papoose, from her perch on a spavined pack horse, gave me a very shy smile through the thick tangle of matted hair which almost hid her face.

One wild animal of the Chilcotin interested me greatly—the cougar or mountain lion. I had never seen one alive till that summer, only a dead one which had been killed in the Cypress Hills of Saskatchewan.

The Indians around Chilko Lake hunted them with dogs, which treed the tawny cats so they could be shot. But they had been so thinned out by this means that I was in the mountains almost six months before I saw one.

Frank had a fine cougar skin on the floor of his cabin, and I asked him one day how he had got it. His story is rather amazing, but knowing how easily the big cats can be held, I quite believed him —I myself having seen a lynx caught and held with only its whiskers in the trap.

It seems that Frank had a quarter of venison one fall, which he hung outside on the north wall of the cabin to freeze. One night he heard something apparently worrying and feeding on the meat. Next morning he took a look, but there was no snow, and he didn't scan the ground very closely for tracks. He jumped to the rather natural conclusion that it was the work of a mink, for these animals often strayed up from the nearby creek, and they are regular thieves. So that evening before he went to bed, he set a couple of No. 1 traps on the ground below the meat.

During the night he was awakened by the sound of movement outside; then came the unmistakable click of a trap and the rattle of a toggle. Jumping up, he grabbed the small club that trappers use for killing, and went to the door; but the night was so black that he was afraid of not being able to deliver the knockout blow properly, and the creature might tear loose and escape. So he went back to bed, hoping his catch might be there in the morning. At daylight he armed himself again and went out; but what he saw as he turned the corner made him dash back, seize a Winchester, and shoving a shell into the breech, return and take careful aim—for it was a male cougar he had trapped.

He shot it between its yellow eyes as it crouched. When it lay still he took the trap off, and found it had been caught by the ends of two toes only. A coyote would have been out of that trap and away, minus a toe or two in ten seconds; but not pussy.

Incidentally, it was a lucky thing for Frank that he had not gone out in the dark, because had he got too close, the animal might well have sprung at him, perhaps with fatal results.

The sight of the first live cougar I ever met is indelibly etched on my mind. And I just simply stumbled upon him, not knowing that there was one of the big yellow cats within miles.

I was coming over Tenas Mountain, on a blue hazy day in Indian summer. Having started the descent, I dismounted on a small level bench. Leaving my sorrel to nose among the herbage, I scrambled down, and part way around, a rocky shoulder in order to get a good view of the Taseko River, which I meant to sketch.

As I rounded a large boulder, something caught my eye on a ledge a little below and to my right. At first I thought it was a whistler, one of the hoary marmots of the mountainside. But looking more closely, I realized that the object, which kept moving spasmodically, was part of something. So I leaned as far around the boulder as I could without moving my feet, for I did not want to frighten whatever it was—and saw a cougar. It was lying with its front paws over a ledge, for all the world like a cat on a window-sill. What had attracted my attention was the darkish tip of its tail, which was twitching in a steady rhythm.

The animal was lying three-quarters away from me, sleepily surveying the valley and the woods below. I could have shot it with ease, but it hardly occurred to me to do so; I am no hunter except as the pot demands, and anyway my rifle was on the saddle above. I did make a very rough sketch, with a pencil stub on an old envelope, for my other materials were also up above me.

Then, wanting to see the big cat in action, I gently pushed some small gravel stones with my toe, so as to send them tinkling and bouncing down the cliff. The cougar never hesitated or looked around, but simply disappeared in one lithe movement. It was as if he had poured himself silently over the ledge as batter is poured from a bowl.

The creature must have been full of venison, and in that state of contentment which so often renders animals less cautious than usual. The direction of the wind and my being above probably aided my close approach. My horse, who had given no signs of nervousness before, snorted when I approached him; so possibly a whiff of the cougar scent clung to my clothes, or else perhaps I had stepped on a spot where the animal had been.

Choelquoit (Eagle) Lake lies at the base of Tullin Mountain. On the west side the mountains rear themselves in peaked outlines, looking at their reflections in the blue-green glacial water. On the east, rolling bunch-grass prairie slopes to a sandy beach. This piece of open country lies so well exposed to the chinook that I have never seen snow stay on it for more than a day or two.

Coming north from Tenas Mountain, there is a point from which Choelquoit Lake can be seen; and no matter how much snow may lie in the bush, the Eagle Lake prairie will show up as a brown patch. Here lived the most progressive Indian of all those in the Chilcotin.

No nomad was Eagle Lake Henry, but a shrewd stockman, getting a very good start with cattle of his own. Instead of following the come easy, go easy way of his neighbours, he saved the money from the sale of his furs and invested it in young cattle; or after helping one of the down-country ranchers with the haying, he took his wages in livestock. He was the only local Indian who had ever been to Vancouver, travelled on a railroad, or seen a steamboat. In place of the usual mud-and-pole shack, he had a good log cabin floored with whipsawn pine. It was kept neat and clean by his wife, who as a girl had learned housekeeping on a ranch.

Eagle Lake Henry had a passion for clocks. His cabin was full of them—large ones and small ones, mostly cheap alarms. But the best of all was a chiming clock which hung on the wall above the cooking stove. I often stayed overnight at Henry's, for the place was clean and I was sure of a welcome; and I always woke up in the morning to the chime of that clock. I don't know the name of the piece—a short, simple one—but when I happen to hear it now, it brings to my mind a crisp winter's morning, with the great chinook arch, herald of the wind, hanging over the snowy peak of Tullin Mountain; and the crackling of the newly lit pine-wood fire, suggesting the good breakfast of fried mowitch and bannock being cooked by Henry's klootch.

My host had about fifty head of horses; and his adopted son, aged about twelve—they had no children of their own—knew the track of each animal in the bunch. While the white child sits at a desk and learns fractions and grammar, the Indian youngster has all outdoors for his schoolroom; and he studies his subjects with as much assiduity, for an angry father is much the same the world over. So it is no wonder that to this boy every mark on or off the trail was readable.

Henry's horses were far and away the best among the Indian stock; for some years before, he had worked for the Gang Ranch all summer in return for a hot-blooded stallion from Alberta; and that horse was his pride and joy, and fathered some really good youngsters. But for all that, his favourite was Skookum, a chubby black gelding of cayuse stock, weighing under a thousand pounds. This little horse became Henry's best mount for either hunting or rounding up stock; and yet for some time he failed to appreciate the animal—but simply took him to be a good strong pony.

Riding one morning towards Redstone, about forty miles away, and leading my pack-horse, I heard a familiar shout from behind and into view came "Crazy Jack" Loola. He was mounted on Henry's little black cayuse and driving ahead of him his own spavined mare, with her colt at foot. The mare carried an empty pack-saddle, by which I knew that Jack too was heading for the trading post.

I knew he had been working for Eagle Lake Henry, building corrals, and he told me that they were short of grub and he was going to pack some stuff back. Knowing I had lots of time, for it was not more than ten o'clock, I was travelling at my usual easy gait—walk and jogtrot; but after about a mile of this, Jack decided that it was too slow. "I t'ink me go ahead," he said with a grin, and reaching from the saddle pulled up a long dead pole from the brush, with which he gave his old mare a resounding thwack. Off she went, and Jack on the black after her.

They turned a corner of the trail in a cloud of dust, and I didn't see him again until I got to Redstone, and dismounted at Campbell's hitching-rack as the September sun began to set. My horses were still dry and fresh. Jack was lounging and smoking by the corrals, and the black pony looked pretty well caked with sweat.

"Hi-ya, Jack," I said, "when did you get here?"

"Long ago," he replied. "Old mare, she go klatawa like hell—no good now!"

"Why?" I asked.

"She all same play-out—see?"

And then I saw the poor old girl standing all tuckered out, head hanging and flanks heaving. Her colt lay resting in the shade.

Campbell joined us. "That mare won't travel tomorrow, Jack—nor yet a week from now. I'll shove her in my fence; and if she doesn't die, I'll kick her out on the trail when she is O.K., and she'll go home."

"All right," was all Jack said to that. He was all Indian when it came to travelling faster than animals could stand, and in being callously uninterested in their sufferings.

Early next morning he was preparing to go back to Eagle Lake.

He had led the saddled black to the hitching-rack, and was lifting sundry parcels in place at the back of the saddle. I offered to take some of his stuff on my own pack animal, but he declined the offer—probably because my pace would be too slow to suit him.

I watched him fascinated. All riders have had to carry bedding or grub on their saddle—but there is a limit. A heavy load behind the cantle will do a horse more harm than twice as much on the shoulders. So I took notice as he carefully put the stuff into sacks, and I will say he balanced them to a nicety—two twenty-five-pound bags of flour; ten pounds of salt, ten pounds of sugar; five pounds of tea, ditto coffee; five each of beans and rice; and a lot of oddments.

Anyone who has tried carrying a quarter of these groceries on a stock-saddle knows the difficulty and irritation to both man and beast caused by the thumping and banging, if travelling faster than a walk, as well as by the constant slipping out of place.

In similar circumstances, I would have packed the stuff over the saddle-jockeys, hanging it with a sling rope and throwing a diamond hitch over the whole. This would necessitate walking and leading the cayuse, and would therefore never appeal to a Chilcotin Indian, who uses his legs only to grip a horse with.

Having finished—and made a good job of it to boot—Jack calmly buckled on his spurs, mounted, and swung down the trail at a trot.

It was fifty miles to Henry's—ten beyond where he had caught up to me. Jack Loola himself weighed about 150 pounds, his saddle and other accoutrements about another fifty, and the grub just on a hundred—a total of three hundred pounds on one small horse. We rarely pack our horses over two hundred pounds—and then we don't trot 'em.

The black won't keep up that pace, I thought to myself as Jack disappeared. Therefore, leaving the post about five hours later, my own pack animal carrying about 150 pounds, I fully expected to find him camped for the night at Bidwell Creek, which is about half-way, and where I proposed to camp myself. But all I found there was the ashes of his noon fire.

Next day, jogging the last few miles to Tsuniath, I decided to branch off and see how Jack had managed. I saw no signs of him, but Eagle Lake Henry was squatting in the shade of the log stable, lacing up a broken stirrup leather. "Hi-yi, Henry," I shouted. "When did Jack get home?" "Yesterday," he replied. "Moon coming up."

The black horse grazed not far away. Except for a repulsive wither gall, red and sore in the afternoon sun, and white streaks of crusted sweat on his neck, flanks, and rump, and between his legs—and looking as if he had lost about fifty pounds—he seemed to be all right. His eye was still bright and his appetite good. Yet he had made fifty miles the day before in hilly country, on a stoney and log-choked trail, with three hundred pounds on his back. And all in a matter of eleven hours, for Jack had left Redstone about ten in the morning, and the moon rose at nine in the evening. So allowing an hour for noon camp at Bidwell Creek, the pony had averaged five miles an hour—and that calls for a lot of trotting.

Henry looked up and read my thoughts. "Me hyu savvy him good cayuse now," he said. "Me no lend him Crazy Jack no more."

I sometimes see Eagle Lake Henry's name in connection with the sale of feeder cattle at Williams Lake, so I know he has done well. And I wonder if he still has any horses as good as old Skookum.

HOMESTEAD TRAILS

CHAPTER NINE

The Homestead

IN THE days of the rapid settlement of the Canadian West, there was a saying that the Government bet the settler a quarter section to ten dollars that he couldn't stay on his land three years. Well, lots didn't but thousands did, and today when you see a prosperous and well-managed farm, you can pretty well be sure that it started as a homestead.

According to the system of survey adopted in western Canada—the same system as was being used in the States west of the Mississippi—the whole country is divided into townships of six miles square. These in turn are divided into blocks one mile square, so as to make thirty-six of these blocks to each township; and these square miles are called sections. Each section is again divided into quarters, each quarter section containing one hundred and sixty acres.

These quarter sections could be filed on at the land office for a fee of ten dollars, and the requirements for obtaining title to the land were at least six months' continuous residence in each of three consecutive years, plus the breaking, or plowing, of at least ten acres of land in each year, and the erection of a house (so called by courtesy) at least eight feet by ten feet. Naturally most of these first houses were little better than shacks. Each quarter section so taken was officially called a homestead, and the settlers thereon homesteaders. There is little similarity between a homestead in western Canada and one in England or Australia.

Since many of these homesteaders were quite inexperienced as farmers, there came to be as much difference in meaning between the terms "homesteader" and "farmer," as there is between "farmer" and "rancher' or "cattleman." The stockman felt superior to the dirt farmers, just as the established farmer felt superior to the home-steaders, until such time as the latter became thoroughly established.

As the branch railway lines pushed feverishly in all directions during the mad land booms, so the settlers followed up—whole communities of Russians and Poles, as well as the more independent German, Swedes, and English-speaking people, who tended to scatter out more.

At the little new prairie towns, the livery-stable keepers did a splendid trade. Only towards the end of the settlement era was the motor-car even beginning to feel its way along the prairie trails, and the light spring buggies drawn by teams of fast trotting horses were still the vogue.

Teams went over the prairie, came back to the town barn, were fed, and went out again, taking homesteaders to their grants. This was called "locating," and a pretty good fee was charged, but why not? Money was cheap, and the price of wheat was good. If a fellow had 160 acres practically given to him, why quibble about ten or twenty dollars to go and see it? Locating, incidentally, wasn't always as easy as it sounded.

I have already told you about the system of survey, but it should be added that occurring every thirty townships are north-south lines called meridians, 180 miles apart. These are numbered consecutively westward from the first, or principal, meridian in Manitoba. Every six miles between meridians are other north-south lines called range lines. They are numbered 1, 2, 3, etc. westward, and are identified as being west of such-and-such a meridian. Commencing with the United States boundary are imaginary east-west lines also six miles apart, numbered 1, 2, 3, etc. from south to north. These are called township lines.

Finding a township on the map is quite easy, because no two of them can bear the same number. For example, take a township abutting on the international boundary line, and lying in the third range west of the second meridian. Any other Township 1, Range 3 would have to be west of the first, third, fourth, or some other meridian.

The sections in a township are numbered from the bottom right-hand corner, which is Section 1; thence west to Section 6, east to Section 12, west to Section 18, and so on. Each quarter of a section is named consecutively—south-east, south-west, north-west, north-east.

So you see how easy it is to find your land on a survey map if you know its number.

I have made a little sketch map here to show the method of numbering the 36 sections, each of one square mile containing 640 acres. The blocked-in quarter shows how to find the north-west quarter of Section 34, Township 24—Range 16—west of the Third Meridian.

TWP. 25 ↑

← 7	8	9	10	11	12	7	TWP. 25
6	5	4	---3--- SE	2	1	6	
31	32	33	NW —34·--	35	36	31	
30	29	28	27	--26— NE	25	30	
19	20 TWP. 24	21	22	23	24	19	TWP. 24
←— 18	17	16	15	14	13	18	MAP SHOWING NW ¼ SEC. 34 - TWP. 24 - W/3M. NEAR ELROSE, SASKATCHEWAN.
7	8	9	10	11	12	7	
6	5	4	3	2	1	6	
31	32	33	34	35	36		TWP. 23 RANGE 15 - W/3M.

TWP. 23
RANGE 16 - W/3M.
↓

SCALE: 1 NUMBERED SQUARE = 1 SQUARE MILE

Simple when you know it.

As you see, there are 36 sections to a township, so you will understand why the homesteader who cuts hay or timber in violation of certain regulations commonly boasts that the hay, or whatever it was, came off '"section 37."

90

Not all the land in a township was available for homesteading. Some old grazing leases remained good, and besides, Sections 11 and 29 in each township were set aside for schools, and were commonly called school sections. In addition, Section 8 and three-quarters of Section 26 in each township belonged to the Hudson's Bay Company, by agreement with the Canadian Government when the Company gave up its jurisdiction over Rupert's Land at the time of Confederation. Also, there were large grants of lands given to railway companies—in some areas, all odd-numbered sections in the township. These vacant lands could be leased for hay or grazing by the settlers, and later were sometimes offered for sale. Since 160 acres is hardly enough for a good farm, the more successful homesteaders usually added to their farms, once they got title, either by buying out a neighbour or by purchasing some of the adjoining company lands.

As the survey lines were only imaginary, the business of locating a certain quarter section in an unsettled area boiled down to finding the "corner mounds" of the section in question. These were low mounds of sod erected between four shallow holes, with iron stakes in the centre marked with the number of the section, township, and range in Roman numerals—hard for the uninitiated to read. Sometimes there was a similar mound in the centre of the section where the four quarters met. Of course the "locators" had good maps, knew the country well—they may even have worked with the survey parties— and were expert at finding the corner mounds; and as more and more settlers established themselves, it became easier and easier.

To hear these old-time liverymen talk was an education. One such, always called Old Doc, would rattle on to a newcomer in a most winning way. "Want to find y'r homestead, do yuh? Where is it? Here, let's see your paper—umm. Nor'west 34—24—16—3. Umm, 'bout ten miles south-west—near to Jimmy Walker—no—let's see; he's on north-east 26—say kitty-cornered 'bout mile 'n' half. Thirty-four's straight north of 27—umm, no one on 27. Oh, wait—there's George Eremenko on south-west of 3 in the next township—25, so you be just acrost his south line.

"Effen you want to go yourself, ask for George and he'll show you; or I'll take you out for twelve dollars. Y'r welcome."

The old liverymen of the West were a grand breed. Most of them were horse traders (or what are called copers in England) from Ontario; and while they soon became westernized they never lost their canny native ways. When I see the word "liveryman" now, I see a great barn on the edge of a drab prairie town. The proprietor is sitting outside in the shade, tilted back in a sawed-off arm-chair whose legs are set in telephone insulators. He wears a grey felt hat, beneath which his tanned face is puckered in the "prairie squint," and he chews tobacco and looks out to the far shimmering horizon, between chats with passers-by. Not that he always sits, for he may be needed to drive the doctor or the district nurse. Even in these days of automobiles, the few survivors of the fraternity may be called on for such services when the roads are blocked with snow.

He knows horses, and he knows his customers. Many a cowboy, and many a homesteader short of cash, has had permission to roll up in horse-blankets on the floor of the livery barn office; and he wouldn't go hungry for breakfast either, because if he asked the liveryman for a dollar, the reply would probably be: "Sure that's enough, Bub?"

When I filed on my homestead I didn't need to be located, for I knew my way around. I had long ago had the idea of a ranch in the rolling country west of Saskatoon, but by the time I got ready to have another look at it, it was being homesteaded; so I gave up the thought of a big spread and decided that while free land was available, I might as well take a chance and see if there was anything in this farming game.

The district was mostly open, rolling prairie, but near my homestead, like a finger thrust out from the Eagle Hills to the north, was a deep wooded coulee containing a spring. So I wasn't exactly out on what they call the "bald-headed," but was able to get some poles and wood, and better still, to enjoy the greenness of the bush and the presence of woodland birds. The prairie grass teemed with small sparrows and the numerous silver ponds and sloughs resounded to the quacking of ducks and the piping of waders. All around me the small shacks of settlers were going up, some of lumber, but most of sod. I had a team of oxen, a wagon, a tent, a stove, a plow, and a few household and barn tools.

I could crow over my neighbours to some extent, because I had my saddle-horse Charlie, as well as a milch cow. Both these latter I kept on picket pending the fencing of a pasture—very wickedly using two iron survey posts for the purpose. These survey posts are just the right thing for picket pins, and thousands have been so used, although doing so is quite against the law. But no homesteader would lose his way by reason of my pins, for I had used the same ones for years. They dated from my cowboy days, when the riders thought nothing of taking them—partly because they figured the pins had no damn business on the range, partly because they had no use for "nesters" anyway. It all sounds a bit lawless and inconsiderate now, but in those easy-going days things were different.

I decided on a sod shack, as being both warmer and cheaper than lumber. I knew full well that some of my neighbours were going to suffer in the cold blizzards of January, in their flimsy shacks of board and tarpaper.

Sod takes more hard work, but one beauty is that with materials so cheap, one can build as roomy as one likes. And so my shack was a fair size—kitchen, sitting-room, and curtained off bedroom—with room for books and a table for hobbies. The son of the blacksmith at the small town twelve miles away was a chum of mine; and after I had got a decent lot of sod plowed around the grassy edge of a slough, he came out for a few days and lent me a hand with the building. He had been brought up in old Ontario, but had come to Saskatchewan with his family before he had finished high school. He was a jovial companion, and I used to enjoy his reciting from the Ontario high-school reader such things as part of *The Lay of the Last Minstrel*.

We had brought out two hams, which we managed to cook somehow; and between stoneboat loads of heavy sod we made great inroads into them with the help of some bread and plenty of mustard.

We used an old broken-handled axe to cut the sod into two-foot lengths, and the oxen dragged the loaded boat to the level space where the house was to stand. The walls were about four feet thick at the bottom, sloping to about two feet in width at the top. The roof was of crossbeams, bought at a fantastic price at the lumberyard in town, and these were covered with willow brush, then dry hay, and lastly sod laid like shingles, with coarse dirt over the whole. The floor was hard-packed earth, easily kept clean. The door and the small windows were set about half-way in the deep walls, so the full force of storms hardly touched them.

A small Daisy stove for cooking and an old Oak heater kept the place as warm as toast. Coal wasn't always possible to get, and it was expensive to boot; and some of my neighbours were hard put to keep warm at times. The stories one hears about settlers burning their floor-boards and furniture are perfectly true. Fortunately, I had a little wood from the coulee, as well as some cow-chips stored up, which helped me out.

The first summer I did some breaking, but it was a dry year, and I got only eight acres done; so it meant doing twelve acres the next year.

Of course, with no money coming in, we homesteaders had to work out part of the time; and some went to work in town, or for bigger farmers, for the winter. Others got some neighbour to do their breaking and worked out all summer, when wages were good, and fulfilled their obligations by spending the winter months on the homestead.

For the first years, this was a tough life. Some of the homesteaders had neither oxen nor horses, and had to depend on a neighbour to give them a lift to town, or bring out their mail and groceries. But the keen ones, in the better districts, overcame all these difficulties in time, and gradually went from oxen to horses, from lumberwagons to buggies, from bachelorhood to being family men. As they increased their acreage they got more stock, and new improvements came every year—a new disc harrow; a new well, properly cribbed and with a good pump—perhaps even with a windmill; and of course better barns and sheds, and then sooner or later a new house.

It was a great undertaking, and the history of it all can usually be read in any farmyard. There is a little chicken-house of lumber or log or sod, and close by is a rough tool-shed of the same materials. Towering above on one side is a great hipped-roof barn, painted red, with perhaps some such name as "Prairie View Farm" splashed in white paint across one side. Separated from the farmyard by a fine grove of Manitoba maples and Russian poplars, surrounded by flower-beds and neat caragana hedges, stands an eight- or ten-roomed house—substantial, clean and bright, well and comfortably furnished. Perhaps a scant twenty or thirty years ago only the chicken-house— then the homesteader's dwelling— and the tool-shed—then the only shelter for his stock—squatted on the wind-swept and treeless prairie.

In those days his household water was pulled with a bucket from a shallow seepage well, apt to go dry; today a tall steel windmill creaks away in the prairie sunshine, pumping cold water for man and beast from a deep-drilled well. Today they think it is a rotten cold job to hack the ice out of the troughs with an axe, so Dobbin can drink of a winter's day! *then,* we had to pack snow into our shacks and melt it in old barrels and tubs to water our poor oxen, as well as ourselves.

I stayed on the homestead only long enough to realize that my first feelings about farming were correct—first that I wasn't cut out for dirt farming, and secondly that a very large part of the land which was divided up into homesteads had far better been left a cattle range.

Surely there is no outdoor occupation that gives the naturalist more opportunity of observing certain birds than that of plowing.

The steady methodical tramp of the horses and the dull fall of the furrow slice become such accustomed sounds that, like the roar of traffic in large cities, they are hardly noticeable, and seem no more than a low accompaniment to the sweet notes of plovers and meadow larks, or the harsh calls of gulls and grackles as they follow in our wake.

The wild things, too, become accustomed to the movement of the team, scarcely noticing the widening "land" made by its progress, and little heeding the teamster, motionless and dust-laden on the plow seat. (Most plowmen have the habit of keeping their heads slightly down to the right, to see that the plow is cleaning properly and burying weeds and trash.)

The monotony of sound, the monotony of tramping movement, and the steady flow of the furrow slices, like water over rocks, induce a pleasant state of reverie, which allows one's mind to be particularly acute to small incidental happenings, while at the same time the hands control the team or alter the levers to suit the nature of the soil.

It was while plowing summer fallow that I first became aware of the havoc which is annually wreaked by crows among young game birds. In this case, the summer fallow to be plowed was grown up almost knee-high with weeds—wild oats, tumbling mustard, pigweed—an ideal nesting-place for ground birds.

As the first "land" began to widen, I noticed a single crow approach and circle around more or less indifferently. Suddenly he put on the brakes and almost stopped in mid air; then with a loud "caw" he turned and winged away, to return almost at once with two more of his kind, who also quartered low, and cawing perched on the fence which bordered the field a couple of hundred yards to the west.

Soon after, the horses threw up their heads; and fluttering piteously, a prairie chicken left the weeds and dragged herself across the open plowing. I guessed at once that she had either a nest or a brood hard by, and was attempting to lure away my heavy-hoofed invaders before they crushed her treasures.

Stopping the team, I searched the weeds to the left and soon found that a brood of chicks lay in scattered hiding. Several of them I captured and carried out to the plowing near their mother, where they immediately froze to the likeness of earth clods.

As the team moved on I saw my mistake. In the heavy weed growth the crows were unable to attack the chicks successfully and knew it, and had been awaiting the time when the downy little fellows would be exposed by the plow.

Hardly had I got the outfit under way again than the three black barbarians swooped down, and in the face of the mother bird's brave but rather hysterical onslaught, and quite heedless of my poorly aimed clods, carried off two of the chicks in triumph to the fence posts, where they ate them in horrid gulps, and then wiped their smug bills on the barbed wire.

After that, nothing would induce the mother bird and her remaining chicks to venture forth from the safety of the weed-forest.

Next day I was plowing left-handed, starting from the fence and working towards the previously plowed land. As the green weedy strip grew narrower, I did my utmost to drive the birds across the newly plowed strip and under the fence to the shelter of the prairie-wool grass and rose canes in the adjoining pasture.

But all my efforts proved in vain; they would not be driven. To carry the chicks over and leave them without their mother to lead them into deeper cover, would mean that the crows, now numbering about a dozen (for their beakships can scent opportunity from a great distance!) would pounce on them as soon as they were set down.

The sinister-looking black birds had taken up their usual position on the fence, each post for several rods being topped by one. They sat quietly, grimly awaiting the reward of patience. As the strip narrowed down, one or two became bolder and slightly impatient, and flopped to earth, walking on the newly turned furrows with the roll of drunken sailors, and keeping a wary eye towards the weeds.

There was nothing I could do. I had no gun. My shouting hardly disturbed those sable murderers, who seemed to know that I was unable to enforce my commands to depart. Each round of the plow brought the final tragedy closer. As the last round swallowed the green and joined the two belts of chocolate, the mother grouse and her brood—having miraculously escaped the horses' hooves—debouched in straggling formation up the "dead furrow."

In less time than it takes to tell, the crows were among them and the slaughter of the innocents was on. Not one chick escaped.

For many days thereafter Rachel mourned for her children because they were not, yet hardly realized that they were gone. Days later, I was harrowing the same field, and the wild mother was still there, walking aimlessly and clumsily among the rough clods—calling softly for her lost brood.

CHAPTER TEN

Spring on the Prairie

THE FIRST faint flush of green showed on the prairie knolls. True, snow still lay on the northern slopes and among the willow fringing the sloughs, but it was rotten and honeycombed, and another few days of frost-free April nights and sunny days would send it trickling slowly away to nourish the grass roots till the May rains.

The first few anemones were already opened to a wind-swept world; and the longspurs were back. The first morning I saw them they were in a mixed company of both sexes, but after a few days the little flock paired off in twos, and then for several days none were seen. That was no sign that they were not about, but only that work in preparation for seeding forbade my looking for them.

In the spring the prairie grasses are full of birds. Pipits, grass sparrows, and horned larks nest in hundreds, but because of their dull colouring and shy habits, little is known about them even by prairie folk, and the occasional glimpse of one of these little humble dwellers of the grasslands, as it flits away and then drops again into the sheltering tufts a few rods ahead, makes little impression.

It was on a perfect May morning that I saw my longspurs again. The male was in the act of rising from a flat rock near the edge of the field, to pour forth his tinkling flight song. The sun shone on his chestnut collar and burnished his dark plumage. A moment he paused, then sprang into the air; and tumbling like a clown, he sang, pouring out his version of the age-old song of love and life. I thought how all birds loved to perch high to sing, and how on the treeless prairies most of them attained the necessary elevation by singing in flight.

Then down he came, tail and wings spread fanwise; and it was then that I saw his sober mate, picking indifferently at a dry weed stalk growing through the teeth of a cultivator left at the edge of the field the previous summer. She appeared so nonchalant, and presently moved away with her mate in so casual a manner, that I concluded that they had not yet commenced nesting; and after a cursory glance around, I went about my business.

After that morning I saw them often. The male was indefatigable in his wooing, and sang on and off from early morning till late at night. Several times I surprised his mate near the cultivator, but never could find the nest. I thought from the birds' indifferent attitude that it must be some distance away, and that they hung around the cultivator for the sake of weed seeds, although I well knew that these birds are chiefly insectiverous in summer. I had often seen the male pick up white grubs from under the edge of stones, and pry around cactus clumps for a small fly which he seemed to relish.

But when his mate disappeared for days at a time, I began to look for the nest in real earnest. To and fro along the fence line, where previous experience told me would be the likely place, I searched with diligence. Every grass clump was peered into, every stone-side and hollow searched, but all in vain—while Mr. Longspur followed my movements with cynical eye, and sometimes fluttered ahead as though to aid me.

I finally gave up the task in despair. True, I gave more than a casual glance around the field, where the young wheat now showed in emerald points of light if you looked against the sun; but surely, I thought, there is no shelter there except at the old cultivator, and a glance sufficed to search around the teeth and alongside the wheels half buried in the drifted soil.

So the search was given up.

But one fine day the cultivator was needed, and a four-horse team tramped dully along the edge of the now waist-high wheat, and stopped, to reach with velvety muzzles towards the rustling greenness, while the teamster went around to adjust neck-yoke and eveners.

It was then that we saw a little brown bird dart out at the horses, flutter in the face of old Betty, the Clydesdale mare, and then alight on a polished hame top. Soon the brighter-plumaged Mr. Longspur appeared on the scene, and in a medley of chipping notes scolded teamster, horses, and probably his own mate from a respectful distance. Then the small boy who had been investigating suddenly cried: "Look—a bird's nest! Right here under the cultivator!"

And there sure enough was the longspurs' nest, containing five gaping, callow youngsters, balancing their heavy heads with open bills, in the hope that food would automatically be placed within, evidently thinking that the commotion around augured the arrival of a more than usually choice tidbit!

The nest was at the foot of the very weed at which milady had been seen to pick when first noticed, and sheltered on the near side by one of the duck-footed cultivator teeth. Almost in plain view, it had escaped detection by even my fairly experienced eye, not because it was hidden in the sense of being tucked away, but rather because it and its owner so exactly resembled the surrounding ground that there was no hint of off-colour or curious form to focus the eye upon it—the proverbial needle in a haystack.

So nature protects her little folk of the grasslands. Let the male be bright in plumage, let him sing to the world of his joy, and show himself in a thousand postures. But let the female, the guardian of the precious nest, be cunningly clothed in greys and earthen browns, streaked and speckled to remove all distinction of shape and colour. Let her have the courage to sit immovable on the nest, even when clumsy humans are within a beak's reach, and no harm will befall the race; and the longspurs, the feathered embodiments of the far horizons where sky meets plain, will be here year after year, to carry on the rearing of more longspurs, to delight us through the dry years and the wet years, the lean years and the fat.

Swamps, no less than desert places, have always fascinated me; but I especially love the sloughs of the prairies, which are not bogs, but shallow ponds, fringed with the long green slough-grass which is so useful as hay, and often surrounded by small, neat rows of willows. They may be many acres in extent, with large areas of reed-beds, and perhaps some really boggy parts; or they may be simply like ordinary horse ponds.

The smaller ones, though beloved by birds in the spring, when they are full of the run-off from the melted snowbanks, are very apt to dry up, and so by July or August they may contain very little bird life. Not so the larger ones, which simply teem with life from spring till autumn.

Seen in winter, such a place looks desolate and forgotten—the surface frozen and great banks of snow heaped about the edge by the wind, half burying the reed-beds and willows. Only the quartering mink and hungry weasel know that beneath the dry matting of tules and cattails there is a hidden life of vole and mouse and muskrat.

But the swamp bursts into glorious life with the melting of the snow, the clear blue of sky reflected in its mirror contrasting vividly with the snowdrifts which still lie in the shady places.

After the dead silence of winter the sounds of spring strike us with a new intensity—the ripple of water seeking lower levels; the timid chorus of the frogs, hardly yet awake from their winter dungeons; the thin voices of horned larks from the higher prairies.

R.D-S.

But the great mystery of the world made new is brought to us more keenly by our nostrils than by eyes or ears, for during the cold days of winter nothing has given off scent. Now we can smell the sweet earthy odour of frost coming out of the hillsides, and a faint but sweet perfume fills the air as the pussywillows open.

Very soon the last snowbank has reluctantly yielded to spring, and added its share to the growing pool; while through the water, stained brown from last year's sedges, the first green shoots of the new crop are to be seen pushing their way up to the sun.

The juncos with their following of brown tree-sparrows and whitethroats have left for further north, and no longer rustle and scratch like miniature barnyard biddies among the willow clumps, or greet the morning with their half-heard notes. The horned larks are nesting, and buffleheaded and sturdy black-bellied plover pause on their way to the uplands.

The stilt people have arrived in their hundreds—phaleropes and sandpipers, godwits and curlews, willets and graceful avocets. They probe the oozy edges of the sloughs and pools, collect in groups on mudbanks and sand-bars, wheel and counterwheel in the sunshine—enjoying a brief period of community life before the pairs retire, each by itself, for the season's housekeeping. Daintily they feed in the shallows, nature's provision of long legs and long bills keeping their plumage dry, although the bulk of their food is obtained under water.

The sandpipers walk along the shore in little groups, piping softly and moving in jerky unison, for all the world like marionettes. They may be mostly northern breeders, pausing on their way—Baird's, Pectoral, Sanderlings; or they may be resident breeding birds—Yellowlegs, Solitary Sandpipers, and such. The Spotted Sandpipers prefer the creek sides, but may be here, advertising themselves by their "peet-weet" note and peculiar bow-winged flight.

The Phaleropes alone take to the water itself, swimming high and daintily, rather like miniature gulls, and playing tag with a zest that makes the water fly. These dainty and beautiful birds share the midwaters with other new arrivals—puff-headed, solemn Grebes; and rather self-conscious Coots, that swim with bobbing head and remind the watcher of hens in a rainstorm.

The aristocrats among the stilt-walkers are not so restless. The godwits sit for hours on the mudbanks, one leg tucked up, the light glowing ruddily on their long, curved bills. Only on the approach of humans or dogs do they become alert and noisy. Later on, when their eggs or young are in peril, they will show their resentment of anyone's approach by swooping at him with a terrified yapping.

The willets love to play King Canute with the lapping wavelets, now backing up, now darting forward to pick up a morsel. They change feeding stations with a clear flute-like whistle, and alighting, pose for a second like a figure from ancient Egypt, with black-and-white wings raised high.

The sad, whistling cry of the curlew—a bird now, alas, sadly diminished in numbers—is echoed from the uplands by his cousin the upland plover, a renegade from the ranks of the shore-birds who has forsaken the oozy pools for the dry grasslands.

But peerless among all that host of long-legged birds which team around the marshes are the black-and-white avocets—they of the slender upcurved bill, terrifically long legs, and webbed toes. Rarer than formerly, they are still to be seen on our prairies, preferring the barren flats alongside the alkaline lakes, where the curled, salt-encrusted grass gleams white in the sunshine, sparse and brittle between the many pools. I have also seen them well north of the plains, in the park-like belt which merges into the northern spruces.

It was at Paddling Lake that I once saw a group of fourteen avocets. While walking along the shore in company with my dog, I heard a loud "kweep, kweep, kleep-klip" and saw a beautiful avocet wading in the water, which was not more than an inch deep for some fifty yards out.

I sat on some dead reeds about a rod from the water's edge, and the bird came to within thirty feet of me without betraying the slightest fear, all the time uttering its cry, rather like the note of a marbled godwit, and continually *sitting* down in the shallow water to probe the mud with its curved bill. Presently this bird was joined by another, coming apparently from nowhere, and alighting with a most graceful tilt of the body and forward thrust of its slaty-blue legs. Within a few minutes they were joined by four more, and the clamour swelled for a moment before it subsided into a subdued conversation which sounded like the distinct honking of geese.

What a never-to-be-forgotten sight it was to watch these striking waders going through what looked like a military drill—now facing one way, now another, and anon running in single file with comical step, scarce splashing the shallow water. Finally the clamour died and they fell into little groups of two and three and commenced preening their plumage. All the time my Alsatian was digging in the sand nearby, unearthing an old buffalo bone, but the birds seemed not to mind him.

With a background of blue water and blue sky divided by a belt of spruce and poplar, the pied plumage and delicate carriage of the birds presented a perfect picture, and my only regret was that I had come without my sketchbook.

These shore-birds all nest on the ground, making a slight hollow among the herbage or shingle to receive the four pear-shaped eggs. This shape, very large at one end and tapering almost to a point at the other, serves to keep the eggs in the shallow nest. If they do roll when the parent moves them, as she periodically does, they keep within the circle.

The mother birds are mostly dressed in soft browns and ochres to harmonize with the surroundings. If they happen to be disturbed, they act in the most piteous manner, feigning a broken limb or fluttering feebly away with cries of lamentation, in an effort to draw the intruder away. It nearly always works with dogs; and a killdeer plover—the most perfect actress of them all—would drive my own dog into a sort of frenzy whenever we approached a nest.

The young are hatched, able to run and to feed themselves, although they need their parents to defend them and shield them from the hot sun or the cold of night. These downy young are adept at hiding by squatting motionless among the pebbles and herbage. A young marbled godwit found by me on a hay flat was not discovered for three hours, though the actions of both parents indicated either eggs or young, and there seemed scarcely enough cover to hide a mouse. When I took this young godwit in my hand, it continued to crouch immobile, and lay thus for some time after being sketched and returned to the ground. It later proved itself capable of active movement as it stilt-walked off through a shallow pool to take shelter from the sun's rays in the shade of a mound of last year's hay.

Once, near Maple Creek, I chased a week-old curlew at a good lick through the sagebrush for nearly half a mile before I caught it. He had got over the crouching stage and was betting on his legs—and nearly won! All the time his parents kept up a terrific clamour overhead. His flight and scapular feathers were fairly well sprouted, and he would soon be out of the down.

There are other birds inhabiting the slough-grasses and reeds—birds which are not shore-birds, but members of the perching-bird order—redwing blackbirds and their yellow-headed relatives, as well as the cheerful little marsh wrens. But still, these birds too could aptly be called stilt-walkers, because, lacking long legs to keep themselves dry, they make use of the grasses and reeds among which they nest, reaching with their feet from stalk to stalk, and progressing rapidly with hardly a flutter of wings. They build their nests over the water, as on piles, and there, safe from weasels and cats if not from snakes, the nest with the brooding mother swings to the rustling breeze, while the male redwing, like a gay toreador, flaunts his crimson cloak to his enemies.

All is not the perfect peace that it appears, however, and many are the tragedies. In waters containing fish I have known more than one redwing fledgeling to fall from its basket only to be snapped up by a waiting pike. These hungry water tigers love to lie in wait near the edge of the tule beds, and all is grist that comes to their mills. Young muskrats, essaying a trip to the "other side"—where something wonderful always awaits the adventurer—will not adventure long if they come within vision of those cold, jewelled eyes.

Downy ducklings and furry black baby coots are in equal peril. I once saw a sooty coot in down seized by a pike, and it looked just like the old pictures we used to see in the *Boy's Own Annual* of a black piccaninny being taken by a crocodile. But even a pike—or a crocodile—must live!

As the desert places impress us by the scarcity of life—a coyote loping or a pipit rising is an event—so do the marshy places impress us by life in such abundance, and with such vocal manifestation; reminding us of that far-distant period in the earth's history when all life began in the mighty swamps. Croak of frogs, boom of bitterns, chattering of marsh wrens, scolding of blackbirds, are but an accompaniment to the steady volume of the Franklin gulls' mewing, and the "peet" of black terns, while the flute-like and tremolo notes of the stilt people provide an obbligato sweet and haunting.

So for a brief spring the sandpipers and godwits teeter and probe, or dash in groups from bar to bar; the coots and grebs splash and cry—weird notes dying in the prairie night; the gulls weave their endless circling pattern in great groups; the great blue heron arrives to fish with a splash, and leaves with a croak; and the rails call wild and sweet from their grassy sanctuaries.

Too short is the sojourn of the stilt people. Hot summer days bring added household cares, and the songs of spring are forgotten in the absorbing work of feeding hungry mouths or leading downy youngsters to safety.

The tules become dry with the autumn days, and even before early morning shows a delicate glaze of ice at the water's edge, the shore-birds have "bunched," and after a brief revival of their spring community life, have quietly moved south to other mud flats where cypress trees take the place of willows, and alligators bask in the sunshine.

Only the brown snipe remains well after the hard frost, to lie well to the sportsman's dog, or zigzag with a "scaup" from his pointed gun. But when the honking hordes of waterfowl from the north pass overhead, he too forsakes the willow flats and grassy tussocks, and the prairie marshes lie forsaken for winter to work his will on, with only the domed houses of the muskrats to show that under frost and ice and snow warm-blooded animals still live.

If had rained all day with that persistent, steady downpour, unaccompanied by wind, typical of June in the West. All day we had listened to the steady drip, drip of water from the eaves, as though Mother Nature were counting the drops of the precious life-giving fluid. With evening, however, came a slight breeze rustling through the drooping poplars, and of a sudden the clouds broke in the west, and a single beam of sunlight piercing through turned the green hillsides to molten gold.

Wearied of the enforced confinement to the house which had been my lot all day, I went to the open porch just as the leafy woodland aisles awoke to the music of the birds.

As though at a signal from some unseen orchestra leader, their melodies gushed forth until the wooden slopes of the Deep Coulee rang again and again. From a grove of slender poplars the hermit thrush, who had been silent all day, now announced in liquid tones that the rain was over, and seemed to invite his feathered friends to "come and see," "sun's out," "plenty of worms." In answer, there came from the deeper woods the oven bird's oft-repeated "teacher, TEACHER," beginning faintly and swelling in crescendo, rising and falling on the air in a steady monotone as though the author were deeply preoccupied—as he doubtless was, for had he not a bowered nest among the fallen leaves of the forest floor?

Then vireo and yellow warbler added their trills and cheeps in a medley of half-heard notes, now far, now near, so that none but the keenest-eyed bird-lover might determine the whereabouts of the tiny musicians. From a vantage point on the porch roof, below which his mate brooded, a brown wren tucked his ridiculous tail over his back and burst into song, throat swelling and body vibrating in the effort to outdo the larger birds.

Stepping out into the rain-washed world, drawn by the freshness of the evening, I took a vagabond cow path as my highway, and presently wandered down the Deep Coulee where the trunks of the lofty poplars gleamed wetly, and knew from the muffled roar that

106

greeted me that the tiny, spring-fed brook was already swollen to the dimensions of a creek.

Every spray of Saskatoon and chokecherry was laden with iridescent drops of water, which at a touch showered down upon the passer-by, turning for that brief moment into precious jewels as they caught all the colours of the rainbow from the descending sun. The early roses, which had drooped their heads all day, now began to lift shyly, wafting their perfume on the air to mingle with the balm of Gilead and that delicious clean, earthy smell which rain always unlocks from the bosom of old Mother Earth. ,

As I neared the creek, the avian chorus increased. "Conkeree" sang the blackbird, and spread his wings to show his crimson epaulets. A flicker, scuttling round the trunk of an ancient rough-barked and worm-eaten black poplar, paused at his work of searching the crevices for grubs, to peer curiously at me.

From his rotten and mossy log by the spring, a ruffed grouse drummed his accompaniment, "ruff, ruff, r-r-r-rrrrrrrr," then strutted proudly on his stage till, on sighting me, he made off—not a hurried retreat, but marching with measured step like the proud drum-major he is, with much nodding of the head and flicking of the tail, never deigning to hurry till safely concealed in the shrubbery. Although his courting days were over, his mate long since having completed her nesting preparations and started to brood, the gallant bird still let the woodland neighbours know that he was on guard, and ready to defend her with claw and beak.

Slender birches nodded to their reflections in the tiny pool, their trunks blushing pink in the evening light, while there arose from the water's edge a misty vapour which lent to the whole scene an air of fairylike aloofness. Too soon the mosquitoes, humming their wicked war-song, arose like an army of Lilliputian airplanes, forcing me to retreat uphill.

By now the sun had set, but his banner was still unfurled, painting the fleecy clouds with rose and pink and mauve, a perfect background for the rounded hilltops rising above their shadows of blue and purple.

The birds had settled down for the night, with only an occasional cheep to mark their presence, only the vesper sparrow trilling sleepily from the prairie level his good-night song, and a pair of night-hawks wheeling dizzily in pursuit of moths, their sad "pee-it" drifting down from the upper air, one or the other at intervals sweeping down with a sound like the twanging of a bow-string. A horned owl hooted his hunting-song across the Deep Coulee.

I came to the house, to see lighted windows in mellow contrast to the cool shadows, a vagrant breeze from the open prairie brought to me the sweet, almost cloying scent of the silver wolf-willow—a reminder that this was the homestead land, where sustenance must be earned by toil in field and farmyard, but where bountiful nature repays not alone with crops of golden grain, but also with moments such as these, to be garnered and stored with our sheaves of memories.

CHAPTER ELEVEN

Harvest Moon

ON A homestead, the harvest for the first few years does not usually last long. The small acreage is soon gathered in, and quite often stacked until a thresher is available, for the big steam threshing out-fits can get a better run back in the older settlements.

A few neighbours and myself, however, invested in a little "Casey Jones" as we called the small Stanley Jones threshing-mills with the engine mounted. While this was capable of handling only a few hun-dred bushels in a day, it could be conveniently run by two men. It was a boon to many small farmers, and saved much waste by way of spoiled grain.

But whether threshed out of the stook by this means, or stacked to await a larger machine later on, the grain was soon put in safety. Then, with wages for stooking being three dollars a day, and for threshing probably fifty cents more, with an additional two dollars for the use of the homesteader's own team and bundle-rack, the in-ducement to migrate to the larger wheat-fields was such that most of us—for the first year or two anyway—packed up blankets, hitched up our beasts, and took the trail. Since I homesteaded in the later years of settlement, it was not far distant to where plenty of work awaited.

Stooking grain—or as they call it in the States "shocking"—is a hard and monotonous job, and usually a lonely one. Except for odd chats with the man—probably the boss—running the binder, and at mealtimes, one is alone. A man stooks better alone, as a rule—less tendency to stop and chat and get in each other's way. It has its compensations, for some fellow workers are *too* chatty; and as your muscles harden up to the work and your back gets over its first soreness, the actual picking up and stooking of the sheaves becomes practically automatic, and the eyes, ears and mind can be intent on other things.

Going out to the field just as the bright sun gilds the slopes is like going into a new world. Prairie chickens pose on the stooks or fly up with their clucking notes. And I have come to quite close quarters with various animals when out stooking. A badger, perhaps; or quite often, in the cool of evening, a skunk out for a stroll; and once I nearly picked up a porcupine squatting among the sheaves.

And what joy it was to take the odd rest and smoke in the shade of the rustling wheat, to ease the back muscles and watch the hawks overhead! Or better still, if there was a grass slough near, to lie in the cool green herbage and press one's nose right down into the smell of wild peppermint and damp moss.

Threshing was more exciting, if the opportunities for observing wild life were less, for it meant working with a crew. It was therefore a welcome change, when one met old friends or perhaps made new. Today much of the romance and fun has gone from harvesting, except in the more northern areas, for on the great wheat plains one man and a boy with a combine harvester can cut and thresh in one operation a tremendous acreage, without the half-way process of stooking by hand. The result is that most large farms employ few if any men at harvest time, and confine their activities to their own land. So there are few harvest crews as in the old days, and each harvester sleeps in his bed at home.

Previous to the combine, the gasoline tractor had already brought about much smaller units—an engineer who "ran both ends" (that is to say, tended to both the engine and the separator) and four stook teams, two on each side. Hundreds of these small outfits were kept going during harvest.

Where a combine is used, much of the wheat is threshed direct into trucks, which take their loads to the elevators at once, several of them being kept busy running back and forth. It all saves time (which is wages) and quality, for the grain is at once under cover.

But a few decades ago the steam tractors were still in their glory, and a threshing outfit looked like a small army. The great steam-engine with its piercing whistle, its tall funnel and colossal wheels, was attended by a proper steam engineer, with "papers," and a fireman for stoking. Behind it was a straw-rack—a tender kept full of the fresh straw that was the monster's fuel.

Then came the big separator or grain mill with its yawning mouth, its tall grain weigher and dinosaur-like straw-blower. It took another man to run this, and he had to be able to put the heavy drive belt on in seconds, for hurry was the word and wages went on every minute. He had plenty of lesser belts to take care of, as well as bearings and other parts; and in addition he directed the stook teams in, set the straw-blower and grain spouts, and cleaned up periodically the collection of dropped sheaves and loose straw which kept falling below the feeder. His was a heavy responsibility, and he walked the vibrating deck of his separator like a captain indeed.

He stood all day in flying dust and fragments of straw and grain heads picked up and flung by the wind, amid the eternal glare of bright sunshine reflected from machinery parts and from the pale yellow of ripened grain. The job put a fearful strain on the eyes; and so hard was it on the skin of the face that separator men commonly refrained from washing all through a run, since it only increased the soreness. After the first week they took on the appearance of Negroes, the whites of their eyes flashing from blackened faces. There was a dirty-white rim about the lips, caused by chewing grain, which they did consistently—unless they were tobacco chewers—as the continual spitting served to clear dust from their throats.

On all such hot dusty jobs smoking is dangerous as well as time-wasting, and there is no doubt about what caused the prevalence of chewing-tobacco or Copenhagen Snuff throughout the West. While spitting may be very rude in polite society, it is, after all, a perfectly natural act under such circumstances.

Following the machinery were the stook teams, which loaded the sheaves from the field and drew them to the "set" where the separator had been levelled and located. This latter was a careful operation, though speedily done. The separator was hauled into place, the big draw-pin was pulled, and the steam tractor circled around into position. The separator man, usually assisted by the fireman and perhaps by a stook pitcher who already had his load on, connected the foot-wide drive belt, gave it the necessary twist, and expertly shoved it on the fly-wheel.

The fireman stoked the fire; black smoke puffed forth, the revolution speed was increased, and the separator began to hum. Up jumped its operator onto the wooden deck, swung around the straw-blower, and made adjustments. He signed to the steam engineer, who nodded and pulled the whistle cord; and before the high note had died away over the prairie, the teamsters were urging their nervous horses alongside the feeder.

When the wagons were properly placed, with the lines wrapped around the upright standard in front of the rack, and the horses cocking uneasy ears at the grind of cog-wheels so near their heads, the separator man nodded at the teamsters, who stood with sheaves already poised on their light three-pronged "bundle forks." They responded with a bundle deftly dropped on the slatted feeder, head forward; and now the sheaves came, well placed, head of one to the band of the last, and the blower began to spout straw.

This may have been six o'clock in the morning; and, barring an hour's shutdown at noon, that blower would spout straw steadily till eight o'clock at night—or later if a field could be finished by, say, nine o'clock. To save time, many moves were made at night; and in such cases the engineers had to move to the next "set" before they got their supper. And to start work at six, the fireman had to be up early to have steam up in time.

It took twelve stook teams to feed one of these monsters, and about four grain teams to take the wheat away to the farm granaries, unless threshing was into a field bin. There was a boy with team and rack to haul straw for fuel. He loaded up by simply driving around and having the separator man direct the blower so that the straw fell in his rack. All he had to do was build his load with a straw fork, and when loaded, drive back to the tender and fill it for the fireman.

So, with a crew of about twenty men with thirty-six horses, a visit from the threshers was a visitation indeed, and meant terrific work for the womenfolk. Potatoes were peeled by the bushel, and beef roasted by the twenty-pound piece. And what wonderful meals those women did prepare! Usually they had the help of neighbours, whom they would help in their turn; and threshing was not only hard work, but often a pleasant visiting time as well. For western women visiting is great fun, and commonly carried on to the accompaniment of ordinary household duties. The children ate separately, usually with the women, for it was to keep the menfolk fed that was the big household task.

Breakfast was usually at five o'clock, with heaps of porridge with cream, bacon, eggs, perhaps fried beefsteak, and various pickles; *always* potatoes, and fruit of some kind or, if possible, pie.

112

The men would already have their horses harnessed and ready by that time, and breakfast was eaten quickly enough for them to be out to the field with "wheels turning" by the time the six o'clock whistle went. At ten o'clock the women drove out to the field, usually in an old buggy, with hot coffee in cans, and doughnuts or cookies in wash-tubs. The work never stopped, but teamsters waiting for their turn at the mill would drink a cup and eat a bite, then jump on the racks of the men who were still unloading, and keep the sheaves rolling off while the others had their cup, too.

At noon—which meant 11 a.m. threshing time—the long-awaited whistle sounded, and at that sound everything stopped. Teamsters still loading in the field dropped tugs (traces) and leaping astride the near horse of their team, raced with a jangle of harness for the house and dinner. Those at the machine or waiting their turn did the same. Many were the wild races to the barnyard, and sometimes a horse bucked with excitement and its rider hung on by the harness, or was un-seated. Soon the barnyard would be full of trampling, thirsty horses, impatiently waiting their turn at the watering-trough. Good humour and helpfulness prevailed, and the first-comers were rarely selfish enough to go and eat as soon as they had fed their horses. Instead, they would put out hay or oat bundles (commonly used for fodder) for the later arrivals. As in all trades, certain unwritten laws were strictly observed.

Whoever was lucky enough to get a stall for his horses in the barn at the beginning, retained that stall. His duty was to keep and leave it clean, and he seldom neglected this. No one ever challenged his right to the stall. It might be a greenhorn who first used it, but the boss himself would tie his own team outside rather than take it. You never tried to get your horses to the watering-trough till the fellow before had finished with it. You always pumped while your own horses drank and left the trough full for the next ones.

Of course, the greatest rule of all was to keep your turn in the field, if you were a stook teamster. With twelve wagons, that was six to a side, for the separator was fed from both sides at once; and so if you started out by pulling in just after Bill and ahead of Tom, you had to keep that place. In a big field this was fairly easy while pick-ing up the stook rows near the set. You usually had time to get a good load on and pull in before the fellow ahead of you had finished unloading, so you got a little rest, and perhaps a smoke from that stub behind your ear; and half-way through unloading, the man next to you would have his horses nibbling at the back of your load.

But it was difficult when the distance to go for sheaves lengthened to perhaps close on half a mile—anything beyond that called for a fresh set, and such a distance was not common. It meant leaving the machine, bumping over the stubble at the high trot, and loading with almost feverish haste, in order to get back in time. It was simply awful to get in late, especially so late that a loaded team from the other side had to pull into your place.

Sometimes you hadn't quite finished loading your rack when you saw the man ahead of you getting to the bottom of his, and you simply whipped up tired muscles to sending the sheaves flying up to make at least a decent load; then up you went and in to the set at a trot which sent up a cloud of golden dust, and pulling in just in time, met the separator man's surly look from his high deck, which was his compliment to you and all you'd get.

But you'd get worse than that if you were too late, for the machine had to run full blast every minute, if the owner (who usually was also the separator man) were to make a profit on his big investment after covering his wages of roughly a hundred and fifty dollars a day. Nothing would be said—and anyone who has worked with a gang of men knows the awful punishment of silence. Instead, the boss would wave in whatever team was loaded. Probably it would be the next team from the other side; and this dislocated the whole set-up, for you would have to change sides too, to make things even. To change sides once in a run was a disgrace; twice, an act of rank treason.

There were other irritating things that had sometimes to be contended with, and made place-keeping difficult. One was twin or triplet sheaves, usually found in low spots where the grain was so long and tangled that the straw from one sheaf got mixed with that from another. If lazy stookers hadn't torn them apart, you were in for trouble. All fast work becomes more or less automatic, and in loading the sheaves you knew just where to spear them; and as weight didn't vary much, you knew what to expect and how much muscle to use in pitching without wasting any effort. As long as you had good bundles, as sheaves are often called out West, every movement was smooth and controlled, with no wrenches.

But to stick a sheaf and commence the fast swing of the pitch, only to find that you hadn't used muscle enough and that your sheaf still dragged on the ground, was maddening; and then you saw it was fastened to another, and that, perhaps, to still another. It all took time;

114

and there you were, trying to load in a hurry to keep up with the other chaps on the higher ground, who were loading smoothly and efficiently. But you couldn't pick and choose—it wasn't done. Once you started on a stook row, you stayed on that row to the bitter end, easy or hard.

Another annoying thing was loose straw, where a binder's knotter hadn't worked properly and you had bound sheaves mixed with a lot of loose stuff. This was slippery and slid off a load easily. In building a load properly when you were standing on the ground—for you were single-handed and had no one up top to take the sheaves—you had to keep them built out on the sides or they slipped off, and all loose stuff had to go in the middle. You soon found this out after you had made a load any old way, only to have half of it slip off on the way to the separator.

Still another annoyance was too small or too large racks. The standard sheaf rack is eight feet by sixteen, and about five feet high at the end. But sometimes, if you didn't have your own rack, you got one used for hay, probably ten by eighteen or twenty feet; and of course this took a larger load and you worked that much harder. Again, some smart lads would build their racks seven by fifteen, or even fourteen, feet; and they had the advantage. I have seen a great hulking chap do this and work in competition with some little fellow loading a big hay-rack. However, the boss was usually pretty decent; and if he noticed this he'd tell the man with the "Indian rack," as we called the small ones, to load high, and probably tell the other man, "Take it easy with that battleship and don't bust a gut."

The worst of all crimes was, when feeding the separator, to let go of a fork which had wedged itself in a bundle. The feeder would take in fork and all in a few seconds, and rarely could the engineer shut down in time to prevent the tool going on through the separator, resulting in a frightful rattle, bang, crash which betokened broken concaves, and an even more fearful rattle as the broken bits went out the straw-blower. It usually frightened the horses so as to cause at least one or two wild runaways with all the attendant excitement; but that was small potatoes to the chief damage, which meant shutting down for perhaps an hour while repairs were made.

I did it once myself. We were threshing very long and heavy oat bundles and I was using an old hay-rack with a rotten floor. At almost the last sheaf, just as I was tossing it into the feeder, my foot went through and unbalanced me so that I let go of the fork. I yelled

"Fork!" at once and the separator man gave the high-sign to the engineer, but too late. I felt pretty wretched over that and was hard put at supper to meet the gaze of my mates—one of whom had his harness pretty badly busted up in a runaway. But such is human nature that I felt the burden of guilt considerably eased when the separator man, cleaning up loose, heavy straw below the feeder a few days later, did the same thing.

Anything that stopped the mill for just an hour or so was welcomed by the crew, for it meant a bit of rest; but anything from a quarter of a day up meant a dock in wages. Sometimes we shut down for wind. Very high wind made loading slow, and worse, tended to blow too much grain out with the straw. You could hear the grains of wheat pattering against the sides of the galvanized straw-blower. Rain of course meant a stop, sometimes for days.

Snow was worse, unless it was dry and powdery. I remember one year it snowed-up in October, about the middle of threshing; but it stayed cold, and under the two-foot blanket the grain was dry. We threshed for three weeks on sleighs—a tough job, because the stooks were simply low mounds in the snowfield and the sheaves took a good deal of wrenching out; but luckily they gave us some field pitchers to help us load.

All the while there was the grain to handle too. This was elevated to a weighing device that dumped every half bushel and tallied the grain threshed. These dumps shot down a spout with a flexible arm, and so the wheat could be directed straight into the wagon boxes backed in for the purpose. The threshermen had no responsibility here. It was the job of the farmer who was being threshed to take care of his grain; so usually he, with a neighbour or two and their teams, did it. It took long hours, but they had a rest driving back and forth to the granary and waiting for the 120 dumps that made the sixty-bushel load.

If the farm was close—say two or three miles—to a town, the grain could go straight to the elevator, which was a comfort; otherwise it had to be unloaded by hand with a grain scoop into the granary, and kept shoveled back by another man—a hard, hot, stooping job that gave one an awful backache.

At 5 p.m. another "lunch" was brought to the field—one of the high spots of the day. At about seven the last whistle blew, and again came the race for the barnyard. Those not having a stall in the barn tied their horses outside, usually to their wagons, and fed them

116

there, hanging the harness over the wagon-pole. This would mean sore fingers next morning if it was frosty, as the harness could be stiff and cold and the buckles hard to adjust. But it couldn't be helped, and we'd say "Another day, another dollar," and go chaffingly into the big, warm farm kitchen with its groaning table—there to eat like savages, hold post-mortems on the day's work, and perhaps have a smoke before going to bed.

Bed meant unrolling your blankets wherever you could be snug. Hay-lofts, empty granaries (hard floors there!), feed alleys in barns, the lee of a strawstack, burrowed in—all these and various other places I have slept in. One's fatigue soon overcame the discomfort of the couch, so that it would seem that one had barely dropped off before the shout of "Roll out!" would force one to face another cold grey dawn.

Some outfits had sleeping-cabooses and fed their own men from a cook-wagon—all rather reminiscent of roundup days in the cattle country; but what I have described will be familiar to hundreds.

When the run was over—a good run was six weeks or more, depending on the weather—you took your wages, said so long, and started for home again, feeling rather proud of having helped get all that grain under cover, with only the rolling fields of stubble and the great straw piles left to mark the battle.

For the farmers themselves the satisfaction was greater. Not only because the reward of a year's work was safely under cover; not only because they had some ready money to pay the big store bill and get the winter supplies, but because every farmer is a tidy man who likes to see a job properly and nicely finished.

They kept a few of their best sheaves to add to the pumpkins and jars of pickles and preserves which adorned the church at the annual Harvest Home, when thanks was given. And even if it was a lean year, disappointment was soon forgotten as the shorter days and hint of snow in the air reminded them that a year was ending and a new one on the make.

CHAPTER TWELVE

White and Grey Shadows

THE BIG prairie jack-rabbits were congregating for their evening meal. From north, south, east and west they came, all moving down to the coulee bottom, deserting their solitary forms one by one to seek the nearest of the many paths beaten on the snow by their kind. From each snug form in the prairie grass single trails converged on those main highways which ran so straight across the level uplands, and as straight down the steep sides of the coulees.

The white animals met silently and drifted after each other in single file in a steady hopping gait towards their goal—my oat stacks far below, where they would feed long into the night. As they neared the congregating point their numbers swelled and their ranks thickened, until they became a steady flowing stream of vague shadowy forms, as white as the snow which they traversed, and only distinguished from it by the ripple of their motion, like a stream as it flows into a placid pool.

By the time the moon was high, thousands—literally thousands—of jack-rabbits surrounded the stacks and were feeding on the sweet grain, which they obtained by pulling single straws from the tight stack base with their strong split lips. So crowded were they that it was impossible for all to feed at once, and as soon as one had seized a headed straw he would move backward from the crush of bodies to feed at greater leisure; but there were always a dozen less lucky to crowd after him and endeavour to snatch a grain or two.

Some venturesome ones stood on their hind legs and in this way were able to reach above their fellows for a nibble. Always there was perfect silence except for the rustling of straw and the subdued grinding of many little molars in unison.

Seen from above, the level floor of the coulee was flooded with light, as though the snowy hills, smoothly sloping and bare of twig, had caught the rays of the winter moon and gently guided them to the valley, to lie captive till break of day.

At the narrow end of the coulee the stacks showed sharply in the bright flood, their conical bulks framed by the fence of warped rails. It was bright enough to see that from all directions the firm rabbit paths converged on this point to form a spiderweb pattern broken only by the darkly blurred island of scattered ranch buildings and straggling corrals.

I was worried about the jack-rabbits. In the years of their normal numbers I almost forgot about them, and I could remember seasons when it was a novelty to see one; but this year they seemed to cover the earth, in the recurrent way of bunny folk. Before winter had much more than taken its first grip on the land, my carefully garnered sheaves had been disastrously depleted, and my stacks were already assuming the appearance of great mushrooms—and in a dry year every straw counted.

I had used traps without number. I had shot rabbits by hundreds on moonlit nights. But to all appearances their number had not decreased. My neighbour on Willow Creek was up against the same trouble, and the Big Outfit—the Q Bar people—were talking of organizing a hunt in the manner of the California rabbit drives.

Harassed though I was, I could not get enthusiastic over that plan. To see the white furry folk surrounded and clubbed in hundreds, as the Q Bar foreman had described, would sicken me. A shotgun on a moonlight night was fair sport, and the many dozens I had lugged home to be cooked for the chickens seemed to be about as much killing as one man should do.

Besides, I knew that their numbers would not last, and it certainly had been the best coyote hunting I had seen for ages, for the little grey wolves had increased with the abundance of prey. The growing numbers of carefully stretched coyote pelts hanging in the shed should bring almost enough money to balance my losses.

Besides—and I admitted this only to myself—I liked to see the swift northern hares rising up in the stiff attitude of kangaroos to survey me and my horse, till it was time to be off in the long, easy bounds that hardly dented the curly grass. Just as I like to see the rabbits' enemies, the drifting coyotes; just as I liked to see the great wheeling eagles which also preyed on them. As I liked, in fact, to see all the furry and feathered creatures which shared my acres with me. I thought of how Seton Thompson, writing about the disappearance of the prairie dogs in Oklahoma, said: "I never loved them when I rode the range with them; now they are gone I know that they were part of all that I loved."

Tonight, I was not ashamed as I stood quietly watching the animals, bidding Shep lie quiet at my heels—my gun hanging unloaded in the crook of my arm.

I had come to destroy. But I stayed to watch with delight the wonderful sight of the white tide which lapped the feet of my stacks. On the moonlit side, individuals were distinguishable only by the darkness of ear-tips and eyes. Those on the other side were completely lost in darkness, but many pairs of shining, jewel-like eyes and a busy, restless movement—more like the nodding of wind-swept grasses than deliberate action—betrayed their presence. Always there was some coming and going, tardy arrivals passing the full-fed without pause.

I shifted my heavy gun. Shep whined with longing for the chase, but I spoke to him sharply, for tonight there would be no bloodstains on the snow.

My dog's complaint and my curt command had broken the silence—and the spell. The hares were alarmed, and for a moment all movement and rustling ceased. Then one powerful buck leapt far into the moonlight and stood for a moment in statuesque pose, reared on his hind legs, tail stiffly horizontal and ears held erect. The next moment he was off in great bounds, and only seconds later the whole mass was on the move—first in a few thickly packed streams fleeing to the points of the compass, with here and there a straying one, who having missed the highways, leaped first to one side and then to the other in a terror of indecision, leaving fresh, soft tracks in the untravelled snow.

Many, who could not find room to flee at once, crouched against the stacks—their ears laid tight against their rounded backs, palpitating fear visible in their great liquid eyes. As the leader reached the branch trails the streams began to divide and the crowd to thin somewhat. When the foremost topped the rim of the coulee, the last were hardly leaving the stacks; and all around there was a feeling that the very hills themselves were moving.

120

Long before the last flitting shadow had disappeared, I was stiff with cold; and turning, I met Shep's reproachful eyes. Laughing softly, I patted the shaggy head and turned towards the yellow light which beamed forth from the log house—white shadows gone, the drama ended.

Mishagunis—that's what the Crees call him, the grey jackal of the plains which we call in English the prairie wolf, but more often, in corruption of its Aztec name, coyote—locally pronounced kī-yiut' or koy-yo'té.

Hunted, shot at, trapped, poisoned, snared, a very Ishmael among animals, condemned to have the hand of man forever against him, the coyote has never been seriously reduced in numbers and probably never will be. Taking kindly to all types of western country—open plain, rolling farm-land, low-lying swamps, rugged hills, or northern forests—the coyote has held his own, adapting his ways of living to changing conditions of settlement and cultivation which have overtaken so many of our wild creatures of late years.

I for one would regret his passing keenly. In daylight a silently flitting shadow on the grass, at night a mournful voice, Mishagunis is the very spirit of the plains. Silvery among the sage, tawny against the grass, his coat seems to have been touched with the very brush that tinted his surroundings. Intensely suspicious, yet intensely curious, the coyote is one animal about whose next move our conjectures are nearly always wrong. He cannot be depended on to do the things which we think from former experience he should do.

He will come to the barnyard on two or three occasions just at daybreak and carry off a hen. Just about the time we think we know his visiting hour and make all preparations to meet him with a rifle, he chooses to sleep late; and after several chilly hours of waiting behind cover we decide that he must have changed his hunting-grounds. That very day, while the men are at dinner and the horses munching in the shady barn, an outcry is heard from the poultry-yard, and all we see of Mishagunis is the grain waving at the edge of the nearby field and a few barred-Rock feathers floating down. The hens, who have seen their lord and master spirited away from under their very bills, are scandalized.

One thing can be said for him: he is no wanton killer; he takes what he needs and bears it in triumph away, neither soiling nor wasting. I have known a badger turn chicken-killer—they do sometimes—and in a single night, having gained access to a hen-house by digging under a cement foundation, proceed to kill no less than fifty-seven Leghorn pullets. Not more than two had been eaten at; the remainder were piled up in a rough heap and partly buried, after being polluted, wolverine fashion, probably to discourage other animals from sharing the meat. The astonished owner, who called me to look over the damage and tell him what manner of creature had done this, later set a trap for, and caught, this particular badger, but the details do not belong here. The point is that while coyotes as a species destroy a far greater number of poultry than do badgers, yet I have never known an individual coyote to commit such a wanton destruction.

As with poultry, so with sheep. The coyote is certainly a great sheep-killer, especially in long-established sheep range. I suppose that from years of association with the woolly creatures he has found out what stupidly helpless things they are, and no doubt has acquired a taste for mutton by eating sheep carcasses left on the range by careless herders. I do know that when sheep are introduced to a new range, as a rule very few are lost to coyotes for a few years. In fact, I have seen Mishagunis trot within a short distance of ewes with lambs and pay no attention to them at all.

I have also had cases brought to my attention where the foul work of sheep-killing hounds has been blamed on coyotes, and the Indians who owned the hounds were paid handsomely for each coyote killed. I hold no brief for Mishagunis the unrepentent poacher; the last is written simply for the sake of fair play.

122

Of course, all coyotes are not sheep and chicken thieves. As a matter of fact only a small percentage are. The great majority live on hares (the so-called jack and bush rabbits of the West), mice, gophers, and carrion of all kinds. During the hunting season they scavenge dead and wounded ducks from around the lakes and sloughs. During seasons of rabbit scarcity they are forced to move their quarters or change to what other diet is available—too often the farmer's poultry, or game birds, especially grouse.

Horses or cattle which have died on the prairie or have been hauled out from farmyards are fed on to a great extent, but Mishagunis has need of all his cunning to avoid the dangers in the vicinity of such tempting provender. Steel traps cleverly hidden under the snow may close with a click on his leg. Arsenic sifted into tasty pellets of tallow may congeal his blood and contort his limbs. Wire snares, invisible among the twigs of his runway, may garrotte him.

The coyote is often spoken of as a coward. Of course, human characteristics of bravery, cowardice, cruelty, and the like cannot be aptly attributed to animals. But if they could be, does the adage "He who fights and runs away, lives to fight another day" necessarily imply that he who runs is a coward? The coyote is referred to as slinking; but is the superior human—who stalks, as Kipling says, "belly down on frozen drift" in pursuit of the "head of heads"—any less blameworthy?

Have you ever seen a coyote hard pressed by slavering hounds? Have you seen him, exhausted and spent, turn without a whimper to what even his dim reasoning—he who has dealt death so often!—must recognize as certain and bloody death? I have heard a hound yelp as the teeth of Mishagunis met in his flanks, but the coyote himself dies fighting silently.

Have you ever seen a coyote caught by the neck in one of the now illegal wire-cable snares? He is gaunt and starved, his hair is on end, and his backbone stands up in knobs through his pelt. His teeth are broken and his gums bloody from vain chewing at twisted wire and poplar trunks, for he has been here for many days, waiting the visit of the trapper on his rounds. And now he waits with his muzzle on his paws for the final blow which will release him from pain. Only his eyes—those burning yellow eyes—speak of a race that is run; but they ask no reprieve.

Coyotes will go through fire and water—literally—for their puppies, but can they be blamed for not exposing themselves needlessly to rifle fire? I have seen a dog coyote sit on a knoll within a few hundred yards of where a man with two dogs busied himself digging down to a coyote den in hopes of the bounty money which would be his should he be successful in making prisoners of the puppies.

The coyote by voice and action taunted the dogs into a frenzy, until they rushed barking towards him. At this the man took notice, put down his spade and reached for his rifle which stood near at hand. Just as he raised the weapon the dog coyote slipped into a hollow, and at the same time from almost between the man's feet, the vixen slipped from the earth bearing a precious burden to the safety of the distant hills.

As a matter of fact, the man captured the rest of the litter and collected the bounty. I was able to get one of the puppies from him, and kept it for some time. But it was too old when taken ever to become really tame, and though it fed on the best that a bachelor's shack could provide, it never grew to be the size of a wild coyote.

One day it broke its chain—for I kept it tethered, wih a box in the ground for its den—and the same evening was shot by a neighbour. His apologies were profuse but really needless, as the animal was beginning to be a problem to keep, and there never was any love lost between my "pet" and myself. I would have liked to be able to write of the steadfast love born to me by this creature of the wilds, and so on in that strain, but the bare facts must out. Personally I prefer my coyotes wild.

Mishagunis seems to know by instinct when he is safe. When unarmed, I have almost stepped on a coyote lying in short brush; but the same animal—I got to know him well, he lived in the Arm River country—was never seen in rifle range by any of the many hunters who assayed to add his pelt to their fur catch. Much has been written about the coyote's cleverness in avoiding traps. Most of this is fact, but sometimes these animals seem extraordinarily stupid, and the veriest tyro may catch one in a clumsy set when the experienced trapper draws a blank.

Thousands of coyote pelts are offered on the fur markets every season, and their value has increased so greatly of late years that the animal's status has to some extent changed. From being looked upon as a pest and a menace to poultry and stock, he is now ranked among the numbers of the valuable fur-bearers; and with increased incentive to hunt him the ranks of his enemies have swelled.

I knew more than one trapper who employed a novel system in

hunting with hounds in the winter. As everybody knows, coyotes love to frequent frozen lakes—to rob the fishermen's nets, to visit an island where rabbits are plentiful, or merely to cross to the other side. The hunters use a light converted truck to carry the hounds. With this they can run fairly close to the coyote, husbanding their hounds the while. At the psychological moment, without greatly decreasing speed, they can let the hounds out, and the run is not usually long. One such hunter operating on Big Manitou Lake told me he had caught as high as five coyotes in one day by this means.

I knew of one animal who made good his escape when hunted in this manner. Hard pressed, he suddenly turned, ran and twisted his way through the hounds, and making straight for the truck leaped into the dog-box!

The hounds, brought up short, were a picture of confusion. One in turning collided with another in full chase, and the two went down together. In the meantime the third had got successfully turned, and ran towards the truck; but as the coyote was overhead (hounds hunt chiefly by sight) he thought his quarry had run under the truck and was heading back to shore. The driver, not having noticed that he had a passenger, thought the same thing and waved the hound on. By this time the other two hounds had recovered and they too took up the pursuit in the direction the coyote was thought to have gone. In the meantime the wily creature took time to lick the frozen snow from bween his paws and regain his wind.

By the time the driver finally got his speed reduced and the truck turned—for one cannot put brakes on in a hurry with just a light covering of snow over the glare ice—the fugitive was much freshened. As the machine picked up speed again, he quietly sprang to the ice; and not till then did the driver know that he had been on the truck. The man whistled to his hounds, which had already started to slow down in puzzlement at seeing no running form ahead of them; but they had got discouraged, and by the time they finally sighted the loping form of Mishagunis, now nearly half a mile away, they were too thoroughly disgusted and crestfallen to give chase again.

As I said before, I prefer the coyote wild. I like to see Mishagunis lope easily over the prairie, or slide behind a knoll to watch me from a distance with only his head visible. I like to see his track on the cowpaths after the snow. And above all I like to hear his staccato bark followed by the mournful wail with which he greets the moon of nights, and I like to hear the answers given by his kinsmen from ridge to ridge.

So here's to you, Mishagunis, the crafty one. May you never lack for marrow bones to crack or strength of sinew to keep you ahead in the race where the odds are death.*

Bubo was brought to me with a broken wing; and his first act of greeting, when released from the stuffy gunnysack, was to seize my hand (fortunately protected by a mitt) in a bill very well adapted to tearing flesh. Bubo was a great horned owl, a huge, cat-like bird, dressed in woodsy browns and buffs so as to blend with his habitat, for owls invariably spend the daylight hours perched motionless against some shaggy-barked tree.

Bubo was a fine specimen of his kind, or rather, he had been, for when I acquired him he was rather mangled both in body and spirit. He was given a place of honour in the tool-shed, but steadfastly refused to eat, ignoring the fresh-killed rabbits placed as a daily offering at his feet. It was wintertime, and on frosty nights when the moon rode high the hollow hooting of others of his kindred could be heard from the wooded coulee which split the plain to the east.

I feared that our Bubo would die from starvation, but I finally saved his life by a simple expedient. I noticed that on going into his presence I would invariably be greeted by a great snapping of beak, the while he glared horribly with his cat-like eyes, and crouched with every feather ruffled as though to frighten me by his size. Between snaps of the bill he would leave that member wide open.

This gave me an idea, and after impaling a choice morsel of rabbit steak on the end of a small stick, I waited till his bill was open at its widest, and then with one movement thrust the baited stick into the red opening and fairly crammed the meat down Bubo's throat. The bird's look of frustrated fierceness was comical to behold, and as it gulped convulsively I at first thought it was going to be so ungrateful as to bring the piece up again. But not so. Having once tasted of the meat Bubo seemed quite satisfied to keep it down. The process was repeated then and there until I thought he had sufficient for that time.

---

*Since the above was written, coyote pelts have fallen greatly in value, and of late years have been sadly reduced in numbers through government control methods involving the use of a poison known as '1080'.

Thereafter for several days the feeding was repeated. I made sure always to mix in a little rabbit fur with the meat, as all owls seem to need some fur or feathers to aid the process of digestion. A mixture of fur, feathers and small bones is from time to time regurgitated through the mouth of an owl, in the form of the hairy pellets we find around owls' nesting- and roosting-places.

My Bubo and I got to be quite pally, although for fear of the wicked talons, over an inch long and curved like scimitars, I never ventured to lay alien hand on the creature of the wild. His wing soon healed, although it always seemed to hang a little crookedly.

One soft March evening I heard a horned owl hoot close by, and looking out saw a shadow sweep silently from the edge of the woods and upswerve suddenly to the roof of the shed in which Bubo perched.

It was then that I heard, for the first time, the voice of my owl. It was no long-drawn, blood-curdling hoot, but more of a whining complaint. The visiting owl answered in similar strain. All night they conversed thus, my Cavalleria Rusticana and his Leonora, and not till daylight kissed the roof-beam did the free owl return to her woodland sanctuary and the shade of the black poplars.

In the morning when I entered the shed, Bubo appeared to have changed overnight, and to have regained something of his old fierceness. Taking advantage of my leaving with an armful of wood, which prevented me from closing the door quickly behind me, he left the perch from which he had not moved for eight weeks, and with the silent owl-flight swept over my head. In spite of the bright sunlight, he headed directly for the shelter of the coulee and the company of his own kind. I was glad to see him go, both for his own sake and for mine. He was troublesome to look after, and wild creatures belong to the wild—not to wood-sheds.

That spring an owl with a crooked wing assisted a fierce-eyed mate to rear more of their own kind high in a hoary old poplar, from which vantage the family could see the silver thread of Battle River, and beyond, the hazy rugged outline of Maskwa Hill.

INDIAN TRAILS

CHAPTER THIRTEEN

Crees and Saulteaux

WHEN THE Indians of the Cree Nation came into treaty, they chose their reserves along some of the most beautiful stretches of country in Saskatchewan.

The Blackfeet—the eagles of the plains—were far to the west, in sight of the Rockies. Under their wise chief, Crowfoot, they were the only Indians who had held their hunting-grounds inviolate until necessity advised them to make the famous treaty of Blackfoot Crossing. Abandoned Fort Chesterfield, on the South Saskatchewan, bears witness that not even the "Great Company," the Hudson's Bay Company, ever successfully invaded their territory.

The Sioux had been pushed steadily westward after the defeat of Red Cloud, and thereafter roamed those western prairies which now bear the name of their tongue—Dakota. After the Custer massacre on the Little Big Horn, Sitting Bull led his people to sanctuary in the land of the White Queen; and although most of them subsequently returned to the States, some remained, and so to this day we have the Sioux Reserve in the Qu'Appelle country.

Their Canadian blood brothers, the Assiniboines or Stone Men— so called because they cooked their food by placing it in water into which hot stones were dropped till it boiled—are also of Siouan stock, and also speak the Dakota tongue.

But the Crees are Algonquian, and their language came with them from the East long ago. They were bush Indians and once lived north and east of the plains; but gradually some of them took to the open country, stealing horses from the Blackfeet or obtaining some by barter from the Dakotas. In time they became, like the Dakotas, buffalo hunters—nomadic and warlike, experts at horse stealing, often raiding Blackfoot territory and being raided in turn. They gave up their bush type of *wikewow* (wigwam) in favour of the Blackfoot tipi.

At the time of the treaty the Crees were numerous and powerful. These were the Indians put under pressure in 1885 by Louis Riel, who confidently hoped and expected that they would become his comrades in arms against the authority of the Canadian Government. It is to the credit of the Crees that, with few exceptions, they did not go to war, despite their condition of near starvation.

These Crees settled down mainly in two areas. One was the beautiful Qu'Appelle Valley near their Dakota neighbours, where File Hills, Lean Man, and Star Blankets are the names of some of their holdings. The other was along the North Saskatchewan, where the reserve names have a romantic and thrilling ring: Seekaskootch, Thunder Child, Red Pheasant, Poundmaker, Sweetgrass, Little Pine. These were originally the names of chiefs, the heads of bands; and so the reserve chosen by, for example, Little Pine's band was simply called Little Pine's Reserve.

The less venturesome Crees had remained in the North meanwhile. They have the longest record of amicable relations with the white man of any western Indians, for they have been trading with the Hudson's Bay Company since long before white men travelled overland from the East to the western prairies—since the days when all access to the great forest region north of the plains was by way of Hudson Bay, York Factory, and the Saskatchewan and Churchill waterways.

These are the Muskegos or Swampy Crees of today. Their bands were smaller but far more numerous than those of their southern brothers, and they have dozens of small Reserves dotted about far and wide over the North; in fact, there is one bordering almost every good-sized lake.

These people form the bulk of the Hudson Bay hunters and trappers. Many missions have been established among them, and several large schools, chief among which are the Roman Catholic school at Delmas and the Anglican school at Onion Lake, and they have been largely financed by the Government of Canada.

The Cree Indians of the northern prairies have always been fishermen, for even those who hunted buffalo did not live all winter on the open prairies, but usually retired into that park-like no man's land which marks the beginning of the northern forests. There they had plenty of firewood, and fish were easily caught.

This park country, as it is called, is made up of alternate grassy stretches and "bluffs" (groves) of poplar and willow. Gradually the tendency is for all ravines and low spots, as well as the north side of hills, to become timbered, until as you travel north you begin to see first odd spruce trees, then whole groves of spruce, the vanguards of the great northern forests. In a line from east to west through the park country are many lakes, and these, like the trees, tend to become larger and more numerous as one goes north, until in the great forest itself they, with their attendant rivers and creeks, form a far-flung network from Hudson Bay to the Mackenzie.

These lakes are the home of one of the best eating fish in the world, the northern whitefish. Throughout the timber country it is the staple feed of the sleigh dogs; and fishing for the huskies is a routine business each fall, not only for the Indians and half-breeds, but also for the white trappers, the traders, and the Mounted Police.

But in the park lands of which I am now writing, the whitefish are far too valuable to be used in such a way, as the country is well settled except for the large stretches of Indian lands, which remain practically roadless and very little farmed. Elsewhere there are plenty of good roads, so the catch can be speedily marketed. In fact, the bulk of the catch of these lakes—the open-season commercial catch— is kept from freezing and sold on the spot to buyers from New York, who pack it in chipped ice and send it in heated cars by rail all the way to that city.

Next time you order Canadian whitefish at a swanky New York restaurant, think of the fisherman going out on the thick ice of the drifted, wind-swept lake at possibly forty below zero, to tend the ten sixty-yard gill nets which his license allows him, chipping open his net holes in a freezing gale, and handling the net with nothing but wet woollen "Iceland" mitts. He has a blanketed team drawing a caboose on runners. In this there is a small wood-burning sheet-iron heater, which sends its smoke straight up in the frosty air. It is not for the fisherman's comfort, which is incidental, but to keep the fish from freezing solid and so losing much of their flavour. It may be late at night before he comes in with his catch, but if prices are good it is worth while.

So operates the licensed white fisherman in the season for commercial fishing, which starts in December and goes on until the limit of poundage set by the law for the lake is taken. But for the Indians who live on their reserves near the lake, fishing time for white-ʃish is still spawning time, in November, when the fish are under the newly made ice in the shallow bays by thousands and thousands.

Indiscriminate fishing by settlers cannot be permitted at this time, or the lakes would soon be depleted; in fact, this is the season when the fishery officer is up practically every night on patrol, for nearly all fish poaching is done between sunset and sunrise.

But the treaty with the Crees provided that they might hunt and fish "for food" as long as "the sun rises in the east, and water flows in the Saskatchewan." Thus they, and they alone, are privileged to fish at this time; but they are forbidden to store up fish, for sale when the season opens, or in fact to sell or barter any of their catch.

In order to regulate this Indian fishing, a numbered permit is issued to each head of a family, and he and his family are permitted to fish with one sixty-yard gill net; but in spite of all regulations, the fishing by Indians is most difficult to control.

Shortly after I left the homestead I was offered a position as Provincial Game Guardian by the Saskatchewan Provincial Government. I had long been in correspondence with the Chief Game Guardian, the late Fred Bradshaw, and knew him well.

At that time the staff of the Provincial Game Branch was small, and each guardian had a large territory to cover. Mine was from the Shell River to the Alberta boundary, and from Meadow Lake to Biggar. My headquarters were to be at Battleford, in the heart of the Indian country.

In my early experiences I found out that many half-breeds tried to pass as Indians in order to obtain free permits. As a matter of fact it had not been many years since the half-breeds had been allowed the same privileges as Indians; but the privileges were abused so badly that they had to be discontinued. Every French-Canadian—and there are large settlements of them—used to become a half-breed for the purpose of the Fishery Act, although he would have been insulted to be so classed at any other time. Since many French Canadians are swarthy, and since most half-breeds have French names, it was not always easy to discriminate.

As for the Indians, one of a fishery-officer's worst headaches is stopping the hiding away and subsequent sale of their "domestic" catch; but we can hardly blame the Indians. The source of the trouble is the illicit fish merchant, who uses half-breeds as go-betweens; and often the inducement is not legal tender, but illegal liquor.

When a charge is brought against a white for trading liquor for fish, in all fairness a charge has to be laid against the Indian as well. All cases against Indians are heard by a J.P. and the Indian agent; and the Indian in court is sometimes ornery. Old Oosekap, "up for drink," listened to the lawyer provided for him by the Department trying to make out that, on the evidence, he had not been drunk. At last Oosekap's patience was exhausted. He didn't like the hot, crowded courtroom. Up he stood and said, "Too much talk. I plenty drunk yesterday. How much I pay?"

Once I brought Blackstar to trial for selling a load of fish in the closed season. He had been up a couple of time before, and the J.P., a retired Indian Army officer, took his plea of guilty. The justice was stern. "What's the maximum fine, officer?" he asked me. I pointed to the page of fines and he read it. "Blackstar," he addressed the accused, "do you realize I can fine you a thousand dollars?"

Blackstar hesitated and shuffled his moccasined feet. He looked at me, at the justice, and at the young Mounted Policeman who was present. Finally he spoke. "Maybe I can have a little time," he said.

"What do you want time for?" glared the J.P.

"To find a thousand dollars," replied Blackstar, who had never seen so much money in one season in his life.

"Oh, I'm not going to fine you that much," said the J.P. "I only said I *could*. Ten dollars and costs, and don't come here again. Next case!"

Blackstar smiled affably at the Mountie, at me, at the J.P., as he produced the fine money from his little buckskin bag. Insisting on shaking hands all around, he spoke again.

"No, Okimow, I no come here again. I don't never want come here; it's Kinosao Okimow [meaning me] bring me. I no *come*."

On any morning in fishing time you will see the Indians, men, women and children, swarming onto the ice to lift their nets for the day's catch. Most of them draw a small, home-made sleigh with a wooden box for taking back the fish, which they commonly put on top of their squalid little log shacks to freeze and keep out of reach of dogs.

The fishery officer, making his rounds, checks the mesh of nets, the yardage, and the permit number. He has to see that no false numbers are put up, and that no unmarked nets or drifting nets are operating, for all that means more fish taken than they can eat, and indicates an illegal fish buyer somewhere in the neighbourhood. No Indian will claim an unnumbered or falsely numbered net, because he knows that if he admits it is his he is liable to prosecution. Any such net is confiscated by the officer under the terms of the regulations, and one sometimes has a large number of them by the time the season opens.

The Indians are a good-natured folk and love the game of trying to see how far they can outwit the law in these matters. I will admit that some of the older men—especially such as old Thunderchild and Fine-day, who both remembered the days of buffalo and freedom— sometimes harangued the younger ones on their rights, and were apt to be resentful; but usually Indians take everything with the greatest good humour. Rarely is an officer threatened, and then it is only bluff, and the threat of arrest soon calms them down. They much oftener lend a helping hand, even if it is to their own disadvantage.

Thus, finding one day about a thousand pounds of whitefish concealed under brush and snow among the willows, and knowing they were put there for the fish dealer, I wrote out the usual confiscation form which would make them the property of the Government, to be sold for the benefit of the province. While I loaded them into my sleigh, several Indians stood watching me. I knew perfectly well they were Northwind's fish, for I had tracked his sleigh to the spot. And yet it was Northwind himself who came affably over and helped me load the fish, remarking that some crooked Indians thought they were smart at hiding fish!

The amount of fish they eat is enormous, and an Indian with a family of five plus his wife will catch twenty or more whitefish at one pull of the net, and have them all eaten by the next morning.

And that brings me to remark that although many of the Indians think that we are trying to stop them from fishing, the truth of the matter is that we are doing all we can to preserve their treaty rights without depleting the fish and game resources of the country to the point where those rights would be meaningless.

The neighbours and good friends of the Crees are the Saulteaux, probably more numerous in Manitoba and eastward than in Saskatchewan, although there are isolated bands as far west as Rocky Mountain House in Alberta, and Rockyboy in the State of Montana; and I have met several intermarried with half-breeds and Beaver Indians in the Peace River country of British Columbia.

The western Saulteaux are of Chippewa (Ojibway) stock. They too belong to the Algonquian family, and their language is much like Cree. In fact, they understand each other as easily as Norwegians understand Swedes. These are the people that Longfellow immortalized in *Hiawatha;* indeed, the legendary Cree Weesakachak appears to be the same sort of go-between with the Great Spirit—the Kisa (or Kitche) Manito—as the hero of the poem.

The name Chippewa is not to be confused with Chipwyan, which applies to a much more northerly race of the Athapaskan group allied to the Dog Ribs of the Territories and the Beavers of eastern British Columbia.

The Saulteaux have mostly remained pagans, and this may be partly due to the fact that they did not accept treaty, but remained independent and nomadic. They were neither numerous enough nor powerful enough to make a treaty with them necessary, and being mostly hunters of the forest country, they, for their part, saw no reason why they should give up their freedom for a chunk of tribal land which they did not want. They were urged by no such necessity as the plains Indians, who saw the buffalo vanishing and their hunting-grounds being settled, and so were forced to take what could be saved from the wreck, including the rations provided by the Indian Department, until they became self-supporting as farmers.

So the Saulteaux have carried on very much as they have always done, moving their hunting-grounds when settlement pressed too close. Not being under treaty does not exclude them from Government benefit, however, for at several points reserves have been set aside for them to which many of them may have to go some day. And while they do not receive the yearly treaty money of five dollars a head, their aged and sick do not starve, partly due to their own share-and-share-alike habits, and also thanks to the assistance of the Soniow Okimow, the Indian agent, who is empowered to provide pork, flour, tea, and other commodities, as well as blankets.

Hunters by trade, they prepare their pelts with the greatest care, and as makers of moccasins and skin coats and bags they are excellent. At most abandoned spring camps you will come across empty frames used for tanning deer or moose hides, and see the piles of animal hair which their women have scraped off with their long-handled bone scrapers. After softening, the hides are smoked to a lovely golden brown, and as time permits are turned into comfortable moccasins, fringed coats, mitts, gloves, bags, belts, and the like.

136

These are often beautifully beaded or embroidered in silk, and are by far the best wear for the North.

If an animal is killed in summer, the meat is cut in long strips and hung on racks to dry into "Jerky." These drying-racks are a feature of almost every Indian camp, and at muskrat-hunting times the bodies of these rodents are dried and smoked the same way. In lean years even the common prairie gopher is similarly treated.

Perhaps their nicest work is in the making of the *wapooswyan,* the "white-skin wrapper" of Hiawatha. This is made from the white winter pelts of the snowshoe rabbits, and the squaws have to snare many hundreds of them to obtain enough skins for a robe. They are cut in strips, twisted, and joined into a rope; and as the skin dries to only the thickness of a cord, the white, fluffy hair stands out in all directions. These ropes are rolled into an immense ball. When enough is ready the squaw works it into a robe by a sort of loose knitting process, using the fingers, and keeping the work stretched on a frame. Often a few strands of summer pelts are woven in, to form a brown decorative pattern against the white.

The finished robes are about eight feet square, indescribably soft and beautiful, light and warm, and so loosely woven that you can put your fingers through the mesh anywhere. Therein lies their value, as the numerous air pockets among the strands, filled with the fluffed-out rabbit hair, keep out the cold as no close-knit job would.

The crossed, bent-over willows so often seen in the bush are the frameworks of Indian sweat lodges. This primitive Turkish bath is used by many tribes, especially before hunting, in order to reduce the body smell and thus allow closer approach to game. The little *wickiup* is covered with robes, and the bather sits naked within, a bowl (possibly Birch Bark) of water between his knees. Into this, stones previously heated in a nearby fire are dropped by an attendant, and the resultant steam does the rest.

As I said, these Indians are nomadic. Having no ties by way of stock or stationary property, they sometimes go on very long journeys. Almost annually some of them go by wagon all the way to Montana to visit their relatives. They often take with them dry alkali from one of the numerous "Manito Lakes," which they trade for horses. This alkali is supposed to be very good for rheumatism and has been used by the Indians for years.

Old Wabanase, at nearly seventy, found himself a widower and decided he needed a holiday, so he hitched up his lean old team and bumped off—sitting cross-legged, as the Saulteaux do on their spring-less wagons—for the five-hundred-mile journey to Rocky Mountain House to see a cousin. He was gone a year; and on his return, knowing he had made the trip as a boy sixty-odd years before, I asked him if he found the country much changed, or had any difficulty finding his way. "All same long ago," he assured me. *"Weechukwasuk* (stars) no change." He withheld comment on the plowed-up travois trails of long ago, and was too proud to mention the railway lines and white men's towns *en route.*

They worship in their old way, but do not consider their Great Spirit as differing in any way from ours. To them it is simply a matter of different forms of worship of the same God, and they think it quite natural that the red men and the white should have different ways.

That point is well illustrated by the reactions of the same Old Wabanase when visited by a certain Anglican missionary, wise in the ways of Indians and greatly loved by them.

The missionary was a friend of mine, and while travelling together we had come to Old Wabanase's camp. He had been saying that it would not be long now before he would be called to the Sand-hills. The missionary asked him if he would not like to be baptized and receive the Sacrament—the Cree rendering being "Holy Bread."

Old Wabanase listened patiently; then he arose, and with the easy eloquence of an Indian he said, "I have heard my friend the black-robe. What he says is good for the Moonias. I am not a white man. The Kisa Manito sees me, and knows that. Do you see that fish net hanging outside? *A-koosa*—when evening comes I take that net and set it in the lake yonder. In the morning I take my canoe and go to see my net. There will be fish—perhaps many, perhaps few. I do not make these fish—I do not put them in the net. It is the Kisa Manito who does that for me. They are his fish and he gives them to me. That is how the Great Spirit gives me my Holy Bread. I thank you my friend, but it has always been like that with us."

As we left the camp the priest turned to me and said, "That pagan is a better Christian than you or I."

Orphans are practically unknown among the Saulteaux, for should a child's parents die, he will be immediately adopted into the family of the next of kin. This attachment to children is delightful. I know a middle-aged white man, in business in a western city, who makes an annual pilgrimage into the far North to visit an old Indian couple whom he calls *Otawemow* and *Okawemow*—Father and Mother. As a baby he was left in their lodge by a travelling white couple whose identity is completely lost; and the Indians reared him until he was ten years old, when a missionary sent him to school, and thence into the white man's world. That old couple just live for that yearly visit; but for their part nothing would induce them to go to the city to see him.

The marriage customs of the Salteaux are most interesting; they have an Old Testament flavour, for should a woman's husband die, it is quite customary for her to marry his brother. Old Kiwip'chikum —or Meesto, as he was commonly called—had three wives when he was about seventy.

I pulled into his camp late one night, and he called for me to enter his lodge and warm up. Within the big tipi he lay in bed with his wives—all together under the same warm robes, which were turned back at the bottom to allow four pairs of feet to warm their soles at the central fire. Meesto was a fine tall man with the features of a Roman emperor, and was distinguished by two snow-white pigtails—an uncommon thing among people whose hair usually remains dark till death. On his left were two old gnarled, wrinkled women, contentedly smoking their pipes. On his right was a quite young woman, plump and pretty in the dark Indian way.

Meesto and I talked while the women modestly covered their heads. I asked him why three wives, with hunting so poor? He replied gravely, "This one on my left—my old wife. Very good woman. The other old one my brother his wife. My brother die, so I have to marry her. She very good woman. *This* one "—indicating the muffled form of the youngest of the trio—"this one I just lately marry. I *love* her."

They have a great reverence for age, and the old *nokum* (grandmother) and *mooso* (grandfather) are listened to with respect. All in all, they are a delightful people and I have had many friends among them. They more nearly approach the ideal "Red Indian" of Longfellow and Fenimore Cooper than any other Indians I have met.

I have today a most beautiful rabbit robe given to me by Kachuk, in this wise. Trapping had been poor one year, and a trader friend of mine told me that Kachuk was hard up. So I got together some flour and pork and made a trip to his camp. As soon as I arrived, I was offered the inevitable tea. This, I knew, would be offered if it were made of the last leaves in camp, and was no indication of prosperity. I casually asked him to unload my sleigh and bring in some stuff I wanted him to have. He did so, and his squaw quietly, without comment, put the grub away. Nothing was said on either side.

About two months later I was writing out reports in the office when Kachuk entered Indian-fashion without knocking, and sat down on the floor till I should speak. I greeted him and we had a smoke. As he was going, he produced from behind the door a bundle which he had casually put there as he entered. "For you," he said. I asked him to open it. It was a large gunny sack sewed up at the top. He cut the stitches and taking it by the bottom shook out a large white rabbit robe, just made, which fell in soft, soundless folds to the floor and slithered out in all its beauty of criss-cross design and bright red blanket edging. They do not forget.

They have politeness. They have no vulgar curiosity. They live in tune with nature, respecting all natural things. Anything unpleasant (such as the settlements through which Wabanase passed) they rarely mention. When they say good-bye it is good-bye, and they walk away with their springy step and erect carriage with no looking back.

But they are not progressive, they are not money-grubbers, they are not pushers; and if anything saves them and their independence, it will be the setting aside by the Government of special Indian trapping-grounds which is now going on.

In all my work as a game warden I found them honest and decent and helpful. If I were sick and flat broke I would much rather be in a camp of Saulteaux than have to eat the bread of charity in a city.

They called me Moosokimow, which means roughly "the lord of the moose." I hope to meet them again, and hear their cheerful *Tansee, neestask?*—How goes it, brother-in-law?"

Since this was written the Saulteaux bands which I knew have been persuaded to "take treaty." I am afraid that as a result they may lose much of their independent nature.

CHAPTER FOURTEEN

Dixie Transplanted

AFTER THE amalgamation of the Forestry and Land Branches with the Game Branch, my duties were greatly increased. It became my job to look after, amongst other things, the applications for title to lands which had been taken under free homestead grant. As well as making the necessary inspections to ascertain whether or not the conditions had been fulfilled, it was my place to see the applications properly signed and sworn to, for which purpose I was made a commissioner of oaths.

At the time of which I speak a great number of homestead entries in northern Saskatchewan had not yet been "proved up," and this was due largely to two causes. One was that inspectors of the Department of the Interior had far more work than they could handle, especially as the time drew near to transfer the administration of resources from the federal government to the provincial.

The other cause of delay was the reluctance of a great many homesteaders to prove up, because they could not be taxed by the municipal authorities as long as title to the land lay with the Government. Contrariwise, as soon as the necessary duties were performed and application for title was made, the title papers were automatically held by the municipal authorities until accumulated taxes were paid.

And so, in spite of the fact that title *could* be applied for at the expiration of three years and *must* be applied for before the expiration of five years, many homesteaders took advantage of the laxity of the Department to neglect to make this application. Their mentality was such that as long as they could put off the evil day they were able to forget that the more years passed, the greater their indebtedness became.

Now the Saskatchewan Land Department was making a final effort to clear up all this bad business, and I, along with the inspectors for other districts, was given a long list of overdue homestead applications to take care of. The reactions of people who were told that they must either prove up or move off was as varied as their racial origin. Some were amenable and quite understood the situation. Others were most unpleasant; but the fact remained, as I pointed out to them, that if a quarter section of land couldn't pay its own taxes, they were economically better off to file an abandonment and let someone else take it over who could use it. In this way many acres of grazing land which should never have been homesteaded in the first place reverted to range. It was difficult and tiresome work, but there were incidents which lifted it from its level of mere routine and left lasting memories. One such seems worth telling.

I was given a list of about seventeen names, most of them Johnston, with a pretty good sprinkling of first names which had the ring of old Dixie about them, such as Henry Clay, Andrew Jackson, Abraham Lincoln, and so forth. All these families were located in one smallish area north-west of Battleford. I knew this to be rather poor land, sandy with poplar scrub, adjacent to the North Saskatchewan River, and thought to myself that these people probably weren't making a living and possibly were not now even in residence. However, armed with my necessary files, I travelled to the nearest town and made some inquiries at the municipal office. A Mr. Corker was the municipal secretary at that time, and a very fine old gentleman he was.

"Oh," he said as soon as I broached the subject, "that is the nigger settlement. You will get no satisfaction there. They live on next to nothing, and even if you do prove them up it will be a devil of a job to collect any taxes; and *we* don't want the land because it's no good."

"Well," I said, "have you spent much money there?"

"Thank goodness, no," he replied. "They don't bother about roads or schools or anything else. However, if you must go, take my advice and handle them easy. They are queer people." I thanked him and left.

The trail to the settlement was indeed a poor one, and my old Ford was nearly stuck in the loose sand a dozen times before I came to the first of the dilapidated buildings of poplar poles (I could hardly say logs) which I found by reference to my map to be the first of the

Johnston homes. The cabin itself stood in a yard full of an indescribable litter of broken farm implements, bits of wagon eveners, rusty cans, and kitchen refuse, among which some fowls were restlessly dusting themselves and two young pigs rooted.

I left the car and went up to the door. As I raised my hand to knock I noticed three small and grimy faces pressed to the window-pane, but these precipitously withdrew and the only answer to my knock was a subdued shuffling and scuffling as if people were getting under beds.

I knocked the second time, with even less response. Just then I heard a growl behind me and the most ferocious-looking dog began to approach me in that stiff-legged way which always frightens me; so I shouted "Hi! Anybody home?"

Thereat a Negro in his shirt-sleeves came from behind the barn in a most leisurely way, as if he were hoping that he couldn't get there in time to save me from the dog. He had evidently been filling up the chinks in the pole barn with mud, as his hands and arms were covered with sticky grey which was already beginning to whiten against the darkness of his skin.

I asked him if Mr. Johnston lived here, and he said: "Does you mean Henry Clay Johnston or Andrew Jackson Johnston, or Mark Twain Johnston, or Lewis and Clark Johnston?"

"Well," I said, "it doesn't particularly matter because I want to see all the Johnstons."

"Well," he said, "that's right. Don't particularly matter, cos I am Henry Clay Johnston and I can talk for all the Johnstons."

He appeared to be a man of about forty-five, and I figured from this that he was possibly the oldest of a group of brothers; so I told him who I was and what I was doing, and asked him if he was prepared to make application for title to his homestead.

"That will take a powerful lot of thinking about. It ain't fittin' to hurry such things as this. We'll have to see Gramma."

Remembering what Mr. Corker had said, I forbore to ask him what on earth Gramma had to do with his personal application for his personal homestead, and said instead, "That's fine. Let's go and see Gramma. Can you show me the way, please? Or better still, come with me." He gave me a curious look and said, "I reckon I just better come with you." It sounded almost like a threat. "Anyway, ain't nothin' done here without Gramma has the say-so."

By this time he had jumped on the running-board of the car, ignoring my invitation to sit alongside, and waved his hand in the direction in which he wished me to go, along another dim sort of trail that wound off through the low scrub.

"Well, if that's the case," I told him, "probably it might be a good idea to have all the other Johnstons, and these other odd names which I think are all relations of yours, and we can get everything done all in one lot."

He gave me a look almost of admiration, as if I had at last done the sensible thing and got the idea; so I ventured to say, "This doesn't look like very good land to me. I don't suppose you people are too anxious to carry on with it."

And with that his whole look changed. He gripped the edge of the car so fiercely that the veins in his forearm swelled as if to bursting and his face darkened into a really terrible scowl; and it was then that I noticed that he wasn't really a Negro, for underneath the dark pigmentation of his face and arms was a plainly discernible glow of coppery red, which was far from becoming and made him one of the most remarkably barbaric-looking people I have ever seen. In a low, very deep, vibrant voice he said, "Ah knows you is de law, but thisuns our home. My grandpappy started up on it and here we stays."

I said, "Of course, it's simply up to you. If you want the land we will give you the title." But I began to wonder how I would ever approach the delicate subject of all those taxes, for while it was no part of my duty to collect them, it was my place to point out that actual title would not be in their hands until the arrears had been met. He was still speaking when I pulled my thoughts together again.

"You see dese hands?" he said, and then with the fingers of one hand traced over the great network of veins in the other arm. "You see dese veins? Well, it's not just plain nigger blood in dese veins." He dropped his voice another octave. "My mammy was a Chewokee, and I heard tell as how dey Chewokees was mighty hard men to part from freedom."

This explained a lot. It explained how they could exist here largely by hunting, at which Negroes do not excel; and I realized that I would not be dealing with submissive blacks but with people who carried the proud blood of plains Indians.

"And here's Gramma's," he said as we came into an opening. And there indeed was Gramma's—a long, rambling affair which seemed to have started as one cabin, and had been so built onto as to

144

look like nothing in the world so much as the long rows of hoppers' huts on our own Sussex farms. Several half-grown, barefooted girls and youths hung around the door. Some of the young men, who were dressed in shirts and pants, whittled idly at sticks; the girls, wearing faded Mother Hubbards, performed various small duties in a listless way.

Great consternation reigned as the old Ford pulled up at the door, the girls disappearing like squirrels and the boys shambling in the direction of the barn until arrested by Henry Clay's booming voice, commanding them to scatter through the settlement and bring the "other-uns." Turning to me, he said, "I'll go in and tell Gramma who is here."

He disappeared behind the rickety door and a long conversation seemed to ensue. Finally he reappeared and beckoned me, at the same time shoving out a very dark young woman to whom he said, "Yo go get that rooster and make the feathers fly." As I walked up to the door I had visions of some curious dark ceremony at which I might have to dip my finger in a rooster's blood.

We went through a cluttered but fairly commodious kitchen into a large living-room, where I was given a plain kitchen chair and told that Gramma would be out soon as she was fit for company. While waiting for her I was able to look around and notice that the floor was of the puncheon type—that is, poplar poles laid across stringers and roughly smoothed with an adze, with no attempt at nailing. On one wall hung a large double photograph in a tarnished frame, of a Negro man and woman whom I took to be Grandpappy and Gramma. Directly above it was a shabby photograph of Abraham Lincoln.

On the opposite wall was a faded United States flag set off by deerhorn hat racks on either side, upon which hung an arsenal of rifles and fowling-pieces, from muzzle-loaders with their powder-horns to an up-to-date repeating .22.

The furniture consisted of an odd assortment of chairs crowned by a very large, ornate, old-fashioned rocking-chair complete with a faded velvet cushion and footstool to match. A long, old-fashioned deal table occupied the centre of the room, and this was scrubbed as white as sand and elbow-grease could make it. A cupboard in one corner and a few bits of crockery just about completed the picture, although I nearly forgot a rubber plant such as one used to see in hotel lobbies, which stood in front of the one small window.

Henry Clay had been standing, apparently looking at nothing, when some small stir in the next room took him in a few lithe strides to the door, which suddenly opened; and then, half turning, he gave his arm to the strange little creature that came through.

She was a wizened old Negress—I couldn't give her age—in a rustling black dress of the stuff which I think they called bombazine, her feet encased in beaded Indian moccasins. A pearl brooch was at her throat and a black shawl-like affair rather like a mantilla was on her head and fell down cowl-like around her face and over her shoulders. She was much bent and supported herself with a cane by her right hand while her left lay upon her grandson's arm; but I doubt whether, even in her youth, she had ever been any taller than five feet.

"This here's Gramma," said Henry Clay, and the little creature gave me a stern nod but did not offer to shake hands, so I murmured something and fell in step. Immediately behind us, as if from every room in the house, began to troop people of all descriptions—a couple of middle-aged, stout women, several quite presentable young women who had evidently put on their Sunday best, and quite a number of children in various stages of dress and undress, according to age, who began to seat themselves on the floor along the wall, rolling their eyes.

Henry Clay led his Grandmother over to the great rocking-chair, where, with the assistance of several fussing young women, she was finally ensconced in state with her feet on the footstool. Then, for the first time, she raised her head and really looked at me, and I could see the years roll back as I looked in return at those old eyes and at the claw-like hands, as worn as pieces of fossilized wood, which clasped each other on her lap.

I knew that she had seen the days of slavery, had picked cotton in the fields as she nursed her babies, and had proudly carried her freedom north to make a new life. Above all, I realized that I was in the presence of a matriarch who was capable of enforcing her rule by something sterner than love when necessary.

"You is welcome," she said. "Henry Clay here says you is the government man. Well, we's had government men here befo' and they're a trifling lot. We-uns came here when Grandpappy was alive and we-uns is stayin' here."

This is a bad beginning, I thought, but I smiled at her and drew her out a little about the past. She told me she had been a slave until Mr. "Linkum" gave them freedom; she was only a little-un then.

She remembered how her mammy cried and her pappy too, and the big folks were gone and the plantation was all burned up. They came no'th to Ohio first, and Pappy worked on the track, but it still wasn't freedom; and she repeated it—"It wasn't freedom." And all the eyes in the room rolled when she said that, as if they knew their lessons.

They came to Canada, and they were old then; but there was lots of little-uns growing up and the Government was giving land to eve'body. Now people said the land was no good; but they had lots of it and there was birds and animals to eat and they had freedom, which they would not have on an acre of cotton, and they were Christian folks and didn't want no trouble. They jest wanted to be left alone.

"And have you had much trouble since you have been here?" I asked.

"No, not much. 'Course Pappy died and that was a sore thing. Melinda lost her twins and came near to dying too, only they got her to the hospital in Maidstone in time and the doctor was good to her."

This gave me an opening and I was able to explain that the Government had to have some taxes or there wouldn't be any hospitals. I told her how Mr. Corker had thought they would not be able to pay any taxes, but I thought different because I loved freedom too and I knew that freedom-loving people were the first to contribute where money was needed, because they would not want to be bums. That word made some more eyes roll and the old lady looked very fierce, and then she spoke.

"Ah heard you, young man," she said. "You done had your say. Now we see what de Lawd say." She raised her voice: "Sally, you go brung the Good Book."

One of the young women got up quickly and disappeared, to return presently with the most enormous Bible I have ever seen. I am sure it was two feet across. She laid it on the old lady's lap, half supporting it, and the old lady closed her eyes and turned her face upward, with the second finger of her right hand held straight up.

"Open it then, child," she said, and the young woman flipped it open at random, whereupon the finger descended like a bird's bill in the middle of one the pages. "Read it then, child," she said; and the young woman, who must have had some schooling, screwed her head around and read out slowly:

"But he taxed the land to give the money according to the commandment of Pharaoh."

And with that the old lady looked up again and said, "Praise de Lawd." And since everybody answered "Amen," I did too, because you felt you were in church; and so we were in a way, because just then the old lady said, "Take de Book away, child," and stood up. "I'se goin' to pray," she said in a very stern voice; and we all bowed our heads while she said: "Lawd, we gwine do what's right. We gwine do what Your blessed word says. Amen."

Turning to me, she said, "You go ahead, young man. Make out dem papers."

It took me over two hours to make out the individual applications, my part-Cherokee friend marshalling up the applicants one by one with military precision. It was necessary, in describing each applicant, to give his name and marital status, and the number in his family if any; so I had each head of a family bring his wife and children up to the table and name them for me separately. I noticed that, like Indians, they had a certain dislike of giving their names, and when asked would look around unhappily from side to side as if in hopes that one of their neighbours would oblige.

It is a fact—to digress from my story—that an Indian will not speak his own name if he can avoid it. He believes that doing so is tantamount to transferring his name to the person he is addressing, and thus losing it. It was customary for an important man to give his son or some other worthy young man his own honoured name as a reward for some brave deed, and he did so simply by addressing the young man by his own name. Naturally, then, if a man wishes to retain his name he must never pronounce it himself. In trying to ascertain an Indian's name one always asks some other Indian what it is.

I felt that, while not so downright about it, these coloured people had the same reluctance to pronounce their names.

However, it was finally done; all the applications were duly signed and sworn to. But I had noticed one young woman sitting by herself in a corner of the room, nursing a baby and with a child of two or three years clinging to her skirts. She had not come forward to what we might call the numbering, so I said to my worthy lieutenant, Henry Clay, "Who is the woman in the corner? Where does she come in?"

"Well," he replied, "I guess Andrew Jackson will have to speak for himself," and more eyes rolled. Andrew Jackson slowly shuffled up to the table, looking as if he felt himself to be the black sheep of the family.

"Well," I said, "I'm sorry to be so personal, but the department does want to know everybody's name here. Can you tell me who the young widow is?"

"Ah allow that-un ain't no widow," he replied. "She is my daughter, only you see she ain't got around to getting a husband yet, but she done have two spanking babies." Which remark seemed to make everybody happy, and they all rolled their eyes towards the young woman, who rolled hers in reply and smiled down proudly to the baby at her breast.

About this time the old lady stood up again. She seemed to have been asleep but evidently she hadn't been, because she said: "Now you got all that writin', swearin' stuff done, the stranger in our midst is hungry and we gonna feed him. Come, you lazy girls, get dat cloff spread."

In a few minutes the poor fowl whose death sentence I had heard was on the table, hot and steaming; and after Mammy had said a long grace and all the eyes had rolled again in unison, she and Henry Clay and I sat down and made a good meal.

I got up to go and put my hand out to the ancient matriarch, and smiled into her face; and I thought I could see a slight relaxing of her grim expression, and just a touch of a smile on her thin lips. I almost said "Good-bye, Mammy," but changed it rather hurriedly to "Madam," because at the touch of our hands her mask of authority seemed to be suddenly drawn over her face as before. Amid a regular chorus of good-nights and the bark of dogs, I wound up the old Ford and started back over the dark trail.

I hope Sally got a husband all right, because she could sure raise spanking babies!

CHAPTER FIFTEEN

A Rain Dance and the Last Buffalo

IN THE heart of the Lost Horse Hills, by the creek of that name, lies a natural amphitheatre carpeted with curling grass and nodding flowers. All about grow the little poplar trees, their leaves bright green in summer, golden as guineas in the fall—ever dancing in the winds that blow across three hundred miles of prairie.

Looped like a bright necklace, the creek divides the bottom flats into many small meadows, and makes music for the restless leaves whose shadows dapple the bright water. In winter the winds shriek through the bare boughs, and the hardy little trunks crack under the crushing fingers of the frost *weetigoes*.

This is a deserted place, and the drifted snow bears no track of moccasin or travois. For it is a holy place to the Crees, set apart and never used for ordinary camping. It is the Rain Dance flat.

For a brief week each summer the little stage blossoms into life, and becomes all movement and bustle and soft conversation, a place of colour and ritual and prayer—I almost said primitive ritual and prayer, but what comparison would that be? Is not humanity always primitive—thank God—when closest to the heart of things?

It is here, each June, that the bands make the Rain Dance—far from the curious eyes of the money-loving whites, who do not see the hand of the Great Spirit in all things about them, who do not believe in the Great Serpents which live in the earth, and who do not see the Thunder Bird, the Great Peāso, under whose wings the people tremble. A *moonias*—a white man—sees but a great thundercloud black and menacing, sees but a great streak of rain descending to earth, rather than the serpent taken up by the Peāso's crooked claws.

For those who do not believe, who have turned their backs on the ways of the People—the Nihi-o-wuk—the Bird is a thing of danger, for from its eyes can come a thunderbolt to strike down the foolish one. But to those who believe it is merciful and hoods its eyes that the fire may not strike, especially if the believers have proved their faith by presents of bright printed cloth, placed upon the bushes.

From far up and down the great Saskatchewan the bands gather to this tributary stream, with its banks all wooded with poplar and birch, with its rolling prairies on either hand.

When the Cree nation came into treaty, the most important bands chose for their reserves blocks of land lying in the belt of the park-like country along the North Saskatchewan. Today their settlements extend from east to west along the banks of that river, which is probably the most historic waterway in the annals of the North-west. Kelsey saw it, La Vérendrye followed it, the fur brigades of the Hudson's Bay Company paddled its navigable length. Rising amid the eternal snows of the Rockies, it traverses Alberta and flows in a great curve across Saskatchewan and into Manitoba, draining an empire of prairies and woodland and muskeg and lake-dotted forest, finally discharging its gathered waters into Lake Winnipeg.

With rich grass for their ponies, plentiful wood and clear water for their camping, whitefish to eat, game and fur animals to hunt, is it any wonder that the native Indians are content, and loath to change either the place of their abode or the ways of their fore-fathers, their own Indian ways? As they have lived for generations, so they do today, chiefly by hunting and fishing, closely attuned to nature, with a reverence for all other living things, and for everything else that surrounds them, especially the elements. So that in carrying on the ancient customs they still give first place to the Rain Dance.

The Rain Dance is often miscalled the Sun Dance, but this is not the true Sun Dance of the Blackfeet, which had as its central motive the making of braves.

This year it was the dance of Wabi-Meetoos, the White Poplar, who had been a war chief under the Big Bear—he who had defied the Queen with whom they had made treaty. Last year Myo Keesikow from Poundmaker's reserve had made the dance. The year before, Two Blankets from Mosquito's band. Always it had been a chief and a wise man who made the dance, and so it always should be.

From Battle River to the west, from Turtle Lake to the north, from Eagle Hills to the south, from far away Carlton to the east, the people came to represent their reserves: Thunderchild, Red Pheasant, Lean Man, Poundmaker, Sweetgrass, Little Pine, Poor Man, Star Blanket.

The younger men came on ponies, the older men and the women and children in light wagons. Tents and tipis went up in a semicircle facing the south. The younger boys attended the grazing ponies, hobbling those which might stray and stealing many a ride. The older people, when not superintending the making of camp—gravely on the part of the men, shrilly as to the women—conversed together in the soft Cree tongue.

There was much laughter, for the Crees are a happy people; much hurrying to and fro from tipi to tipi, renewing acquaintances with usually far-distant friends. Much admiring of new babies with their solemn black eyes, straight hair and dusky red cheeks, like to ours in their chubby lovableness. Much gossip and much sly lovemaking, and therefore much singing, for when a Cree youth is in love he rides about the outskirts of the camp and raises his voice in a monotonous and yet musical chant, apparently to the world at large. Nobody pays any attention to him; but the maiden of his choice knows, though she would rather die than lift her head from the cooking-fire to steal a look.

But most of the people were engaged in erecting the great dance lodge in the centre of the amphitheatre. Some cut poplars in the adjoining groves, some hauled the felled trees, branches and all, to the site by means of ropes and ponies; others peeled and trimmed and set the poles up. Soon it was completed. It was roomy and circular, the roof supported by a great central pole to the top of which had been attached bright ribbons and a piece of a mirror as a compliment to the revered Sun. Peeled poles were fastened like spokes from the central upright to the outside walls, also of poles. The whole was covered, bower-like, with poplar branches on which the green leaves rustled and trembled. Breast-high stalls of similar green boughs were provided within for the dancers.

That night the pipe was passed and the dancing commenced, but not before the old ones had, in turn, raised their faces to the Father of Life, asking for His blessing of rain and fertility. The air was heavy with the resonance of the drums, beaten with the flat of the hand. The piping of the dancers was weird and melancholy. The four chosen ones danced within the stalls, stripped to the waist. As they bobbed up and down, the sweat streaked the ochre of their cheeks.

The dancing consisted of lifting the moccasined feet alternately without any change of place or position. In their mouths they held decorated whistles made from the hollow wing-bones of geese. Through these they piped at every breath a high, monotonous note. A small fire burnt in the centre of the lodge, but not for warmth. The spring had been dry and hot, and no respite seemed in sight for the parched land.

As the dancing continued, the chief participants ate no food, nor drank, nor desisted from motion, were it ever so slight. To the farmers in the settlements, the sound of drumming was born on the dry wind. "The Indians are dancing," said one to another and "Perhaps we shall have rain," added some.

The evening of the third day came and Wabi-Meetoos addressed the people—the grave chiefs and councillors who sat within the lodge, the younger men in groups outside, the women whose gay head kerchiefs made brighter colour in the dusk.

He spoke of the past, of the ways of their people in the days gone by when buffalo were plentiful, of the days before the white man had eaten all but a fraction of their inheritance. He spoke of the present. Why did the people try to be like the white man—or worse, like the half-breeds who so often stole the offerings left on the bushes for the

Peāso? Too many of the young men had cut their hair. That was not good. Without their plaited braids (he shook his) they were like eagles without feathers. They looked like half-breeds, and the Keesa-Manitoo would not know them. No wonder the land was dry, and the grass was thin!

He spoke of the future. He was old, very old, and his brothers here—indicating the chiefs—were old. The rule of the *Moonias* was good, he had no complaint. But there were things the white men did not know. They believed the Great Peāso was only a cloud. They did not believe in the Great Serpents whose dens were in the creek banks. Thy talked about the Manitoo, but they did not believe in His power, because they were blinded by their own. In the name of their Manitoo they talked of giving, but it was only talk, for even while their tongues spoke their hands seized.

If the young men did not remain true to their ways, many things would be forgotten—in time, perhaps, the very tongue in which he spoke—and the Keesa-Manitoo would cover His face. Who would make the dances after he and these old ones were taken to the Sand-hills?

Tapwa (in truth) they should be reminded of many things, and he would tell them again of Wee-sah-ka-chak, the Worldmaker, that they might be humbled and remember that man had not made the world and man could not bring rain by wishing for it.

Wabi-Meetoos paused. All eyes were upon him, but he, as if for inspiration, turned his face a moment to the sky, visible through the leafy panoply above. No stars twinkled as on previous nights. It was overcast.

"Long ago," he said, drawing his blanket more closely about his lean old shoulders, "long ago the land was covered with water. It was all covered with water. Then came Wee-sah-ka-chak, the Worldmaker. Then came he, singing in his canoe. And with him were his brothers the animals—the Beaver, the Muskrat, the Coyote, the Badger, the Bear, the Deer and the Duck and the Crow, all the birds and all the animals had he with him. Wee-sah-ka-chak came to make the world for the Crees.

"First he sent the Beaver out to dive. But the Beaver soon came up for breath. Then he chose the Muskrat saying: 'O Wutchusk, you are small, but you can swim and dive, none better. Go down in the water, that you may bring me some mud that I may build a home for all.'

"So the Muskrat dived, and when he came back, lo, he held in his front paws some mud. Then Wee-sah-ka-chak took this and held it in his hands, and he blew mightily upon it so that the sound was like the rushing of the north-west winds through the pine trees. And the mud became with his blowing larger and larger until at last the canoe was on dry land and not any water could be seen by the eyes of Wee-sah-ka-chak.

"Then did he send O-ho-suh, the Crow, out to fly, bidding him return only when he had circled the earth. But in two days the Crow returned. Then Wee-sah-ka-chak blew again upon the earth, and this time it was as if a blizzard were driving the snow like sand in the country of the Blackfeet. Now he sent out the Rabbit, bidding him also to return when he had seen all of the earth. And presently the Rabbit also returned. Wee-sah-ka-chak blew again, so mightily that this time the noise was like unto the guns of the Mishi-Mokomanuk when they battle.

"Then spake Wee-sah-ka-chak to Mishuganis, the Coyote, saying, 'O Mishuganis, you are a coward and cunning, and you can run far without eating. Go then as the others went, and if you come not back, then shall Wee-sah-ka-chak know that his world is large enough.' And so the Coyote ran over the earth with his tail between his legs, and he came not back.

"Thus was the manner of the making of the world. My father told me, and his father told him, and his father's father told his father. It was so, and I have finished speaking to you, my brothers and my children."

Again the White Poplar paused and looked upward. The air was still. The people were silent. There came a soft pattering on the leafy ceiling of the lodge, but only for a moment, then all was still again. The old chief motioned to the squatting drummers, who brought their hands down sharply. As the tight drumskins responded there was an answering roar of steady rain from outside. The dancers piped shrilly. The Keesa-Manitoo had answered.

Far off beyond the hills, far over the plains where the white man farmed, the lightning danced and played; danced like a prairie fire on the rim of the world. But here was steady, welcome rain, for the Great Spirit had heard his people, and the great and terrible Thunder Bird had seen the offerings bright and new upon the bushes, and had shielded his eyes in the direction of the dance lodge.

With the coming of the rain the dance was over. The tired participants gratefully accepted food and rest. The old people conversed in groups while the rain dripped steadily from tipi flaps and poplar trees. The young men spoke quietly together, trying to catch the eyes of their chosen ones, who dropped their glances and laughed musically because they were happy. From this meeting of the bands many marriages would come, and that, the old ones agreed, was good.

Long before the morning sun touched the hilltops, the cooking-fires sent up their blue wreaths, and by noon the last pony had been urged up the rutted trail that wound out through the hills.

With only the print offerings, hanging still wet on the bushes, to hint at the finery of the young men, and only the rippling creek to echo the laughter of the girls, the Rain Dance flat lay deserted.

I was on a game patrol in the sand-hills north of Little Pine's Reserve, and as noon approached I swung through the long willow draw to Makwa Lake, where I could water my horse and enjoy my lunch by the blue waters.

But someone was ahead of me, for near the shore I saw a hobbled team grazing, and presently came upon a wagon. A thin wisp of smoke curled up from a sheltered hollow, and I saw it was my friend Old Owstichow, who was feeding the fire with small willows.

His kindly dark face wrinkled into a smile as he greeted me with a dignified handshake. I turned my horse loose to graze, and we lunched together. He had been away, he said, to visit his married daughter at Onion Lake. During our chat my horse strayed out of sight behind a knoll, so I went after him for fear he might go too far. Bringing him back to camp, I stumbled upon an old buffalo skull in exceptionally good condition, considering that it must have lain exposed to the rigours of prairie weather for well on to fifty years.

I carried this to camp, with the idea of asking Old Owstichow to take it in his wagon and drop it at the house of a friend of mine for safe-keeping until such time as I could collect it and take it home.

Now I turned it over in my hand for a further inspection, picking curiously at it with my pocket-knife. It was then that I noticed my Cree companion peering also at the bleached skull with a curiously intent expression. *"Moostoos,"* he said softly, and drew on his pipe while his eyes narrowed thoughtfully. I knew a question was coming.

Owstichow turned to me. "Is it true," he said in soft Cree, "Is it true, Okimowsis, as I have heard said, that in the country west of the Blackfoot Hills there are many buffalo still living?"

"Yes," I replied, and told him as best I could the story of how the Canadian Government had purchased the last surviving band of plains buffalo from Michael Pablo, the Montana half-breed; and how these buffalo had for many years now been confined in a big fenced range over west in Alberta.

Owstichow listened gravely. "They spoke the truth then, my friends who told me this." He paused and again pulled on his pipe. "But you say they are behind a fence? And the Government will not allow them to be hunted? Of what use, then, are they?"

This was beyond me. How could I explain the white man's sentiment to one of a race who believed that all creatures were put here by the Keesa-Manitoo to be the Indians' food and clothing?

I knew he had killed buffalo in his youth, and to change the subject asked him casually how many he had killed and whether he would kill a buffalo again, if he knew it to be the last.

He grunted a Cree affirmative. "For," he added, "the *moostoosuk* were for the red man, and it would be right that the last should die by the hand of the red man. The land was always the red man's, the buffalo his. The *moonias* has the land now—should he also have the buffalo? What need has he of the meat and hides, when his own cattle are as many as the leaves, and he himself grows fat on *pewabsk-wis-o-weash* (canned food)?"

"*Tapwa*, the Manitoo has gathered the buffalo to Him, that they might provide food for the Nihiowuk in the Great Sand-hills of the spirit world."

"Your words are strong, Owstichow," I said, curiously nettled, for there was meat in his reasoning.

"Not only my words, Okimowsis," he replied, "but once this body, too, was strong. Once it was young, and I hunted the last buffaloes—nay, I *killed* the last of them. By my hand he died, and, knowing it was the last, I did not stay my hand."

His voice had begun to take on the sonorous ring of the Indian orator; and hoping he would continue, and fearing that he might reassume that mark of indifference so usual to him, I questioned him no further, and looked no more at him. Instead, I gazed over the rolling expanse of brush and prairie which slopes to the sparkling water of Battle River. To the west, a faint blue line on the horizon, lay the Blackfoot Hills.

As I had hoped, the old Cree continued to speak; and as he spoke in the short, deliberate sentences, punctuated by long, dramatic pauses, as is the Indian way, I fancied I could see bulky forms rise grunting to their knees, then break into a clumsy gallop, weaving in and out of the poplar bluffs in a dusty haze.

It was two—maybe three years before the Thirst Dance of Big Bear, when we foolish ones sought to drive back the soldiers of the Okimowskwā—the good white Queen—[Owstichow referred to the rebellion of '85.] The buffalo had all been killed, they said. Everywhere the story was the same. The Stoneys of the South were starving. The Blackfeet of the West were being fed by the Police. The Sioux faced famine. The Mishi-Mokomanuk, they said, led by the chief with yellow hair, had even poisoned the buffalo—to force the Indians back on their reserves.

We only, the Crees of the North, were able to live, because the Manitoo had given us deer and moose, and fish also. Not so good as buffalo, but better than the lean rabbits that stewed in the lodges to the south. And we had a secret—three of us, Arrow-boy, First Sky, and I, Owstichow, the-man-who-has-a-purpose. And the secret was this—that in a valley of the Blackfoot hills, seldom straying far, there lived still some buffalo—sixteen or more.

I had seen them, counted them roughly, that spring when I was looking for the pinto mare which was the grandmother of the mare I ride today. I forbore to shoot one. My camp was far distant. No trees grew for travois poles, and I could not haul the meat. First Sky and Arrow-boy, on their way back from Frog Lake, saw the tracks later near the Thunder Coulee. We three spoke to no one of these buffalo.

But one day First Sky told us that white men were travelling north-west from Pile of Bones Creek to hunt buffalo. So we left our camp on Birch Lake and travelled west. We desired to kill those buffalo ourselves. For three days we travelled, mounted on our best ponies. We knew our women would find our trail, and follow with the travois ponies. On the fourth day we reached Thunder Coulee. After resting ourselves and our ponies, we went out to look for buffalo.

Arrow-boy rode north. First Sky rode south. I rode west. We rode in a circle from left to right. All that day I rode but saw no buffalo. As I returned to camp, I saw First Sky riding over a ridge. When he saw me he made the buffalo sign, and I knew we would hunt the next day.

In camp, First Sky told us that seventeen buffalo were feeding

158

on the flats south of Battle River, near the Sounding Lake trail. Early next morning we got up, mounted our horses, and rode south-west. Just across the river were some rolling hills, and beyond them a plain.

First Sky rode ahead and peeped over a ridge. While we watched, he put his hands to his head in the sign. He then rode back and told us that the buffalo were moving west towards the broken country. We then rode up a small coulee which opened onto the plain. As soon as the buffalo saw us they began to run, but our ponies were strong and fresh. One by one, we rode alongside and shot them with our muskets. The very last was a large bull. He headed south across the plain, and had a good start. First Sky and Arrow-boy had already left their ponies to start skinning. I put my horse to his best speed. As I came near, the bull turned slightly as if about to face me. When I saw his eyes I called, "Brother, I need you." He turned again, and I whipped my horse. Pretty soon I came close to the bull, and fired my musket, aiming behind his shoulder. He stumbled and ran on a bit, and then fell on his side, and I had to stop quickly or fall over him.

Thus he died—the last buffalo. Ākoosā, it is well.

While we were skinning, we saw the women coming slowly towards us. They had been to our camping-place, and then, hearing the shooting, had come.

They made the pemmican and in about two weeks we started back for the Battleford country with loaded travois. Near the Eye-hill Creek we met some white hunters with half-breed guides. We stopped and talked. The white men gave us tobacco and tried to buy pemmican. But we would not sell any, only gave them some. One of the half-breeds said, "Look, this pemmican is fresh made. They have been killing Buffalo—perhaps those last buffalo the Police told about, which we were going to hunt." He said this in Cree to the other half-breed, who seemed to tell it to one of the white men.

This white man was tall and straight, and I afterwards heard he was a big Okimow who came from the East to make an iron road for the Queen. He said something in his own tongue, and the half-breed laughed. I asked what the Okimow had said. The half-breed replied, "He said that if you Indians have killed the last of the buffalo, he does not see who has a better right."

For those words I liked that white man.

But that was long ago, and now my people are like the buffalo you tell me about—fenced around, and the old ones fed by the Soniow-Okimow. Like the buffalo they are gone from the country of grass, and their camp-fires are lost under the weeds even as the bones of this one you hold. Their smoke cannot rise above the wheat fields.

As Owstichow finished, I rubbed my eyes. Gone were the riders, gone the brown buffalo. I saw only a strip of rolling prairie, too sandy to be plowed; only a gleam of water; only a dried and bleached old skull.

Quietly I carried the skull back to the dint in the sod from which I had pried it, coaxing the grass over it in half concealment. It was out of respect for the reverence which Indians give to the bones and antlers of game animals.

Quietly we parted—Owstichow, the-man-with-a-purpose, and I, the *moonias,* one of those who now replaced his race as lords of the prairies.

Gordon Hewitt in his *The Conservation of the Wild Life of Canada* gives 1883 as the last year in which plains buffalo were seen in Canada. This was in Saskatchewan. He states that in that year a few pounds of fresh pemmican found its way to Winnipeg. He quotes Professor Kenaston, who met a party of Englishmen hunting buffalo on Battle River in 1881. There may be some connection between this and Owstichow's story; although if this was the party the Indians met, my friend must have been wrong in his dates, and also in thinking that he had killed the last buffalo.

I am inclined to think that Owstichow was right and that the year was '83, two years before the rebellion, and that these *were* the last buffalo, possibly the remnants of the band which Kenaston's Englishmen had hunted. Kenaston himself was over the same ground in 1883, exploring for the C.P.R. (the White Queen to an Indian), and may have been the white man to whom Owstichow took a liking.

NORTHERN TRAILS

CHAPTER SIXTEEN

The Ranger Station

WHEN I was sent on duty to the North, the Game and Fishery Branch had already been merged with Forestry to form one department, and thereafter the officers had the care of forests and game together.

I was posted to a large forest and game reserve which embraces most of the Pasquia hills of north-east Saskatchewan. The nearest town is The Pas, in Manitoba, famous as a jumping-off place for Hudson Bay. Fully living up to the slogan "The Friendly North," it welcomes everybody, and is a great meeting-place for fur buyers.

From The Pas—or, to give it its old French name, Le Pas—if you look westward you can see what they call the Pasquia "Mountain" lying blue in the distance, although in truth this is no mountain even if it is the first considerable rise of land west of Lake Winnipeg. The Pas itself is on the first prairie level, or steppe, further south on which lie the wheat plains of Red River and Portage la Prairie. The hills rise from the 900-foot level of the plain to roughly 1500 or 2000 feet, the highest point being about 2200, and the distant blue line is the eastern escarpment of the second prairie level, an escarpment which can be traced south along the Porcupine Hills, the Riding Mountains, and the Turtle Hills. But on the west side the hills drop comparatively little, carrying on gradually to the general 1500-foot level of the country beyond.

This is a country of much more rainfall than south or central Saskatchewan, and therefore very heavily timbered in most spots, although there are large areas of flat hay meadows subject to flooding, as well as extensive muskegs. It is the heart of the marketable timber area of the North-west east of the Rockies, and so The Pas is not only a fur centre, but the location of one of the largest sawmills in the country. This has extensive timber tracts up the Saskatchewan towards Cumberland House, as well as up the Carrot River north of the hills, and in the Porcupine Hills to the south-west.

There is practically no farming done, except along the meadows west of the town, where a few farmers have established themselves. Trapping is the main occupation of Indians, half-breeds, and whites alike.

The Pasquia hills are very difficult to travel in, and have practically no trails. It was proposed to attempt regular patrols to keep down poaching, for such had been the competition for furs that all fur-bearers were getting really scarce. It was hoped to build up a reservoir of wildlife from which the overflow would probably benefit the surrounding country.

The area also included several townships next to the western border of Manitoba, and east of the hills, in the flat, low-lying lake-and-meadow country through which the Pasquia River takes the gathered-up waters of the Waskwei and its tributaries into Manitoba, to join the Saskatchewan near The Pas. The Forestry people had for some years maintained Rangers at various points—along the Carrot River, for example—and it was one of these ranger stations that was to be my home.

The cabin stood in a clearing. Not a large clearing, but its grassy opening afforded relief from the monotony of the forty-foot green wall that surrounded it on three sides. On the fourth was the river, also green, reflecting the overhanging spruce and poplar, and winding so tortuously through the breathless forest that this tiny opening on its bank could not be seen until one's canoe touched the bleached logs that, fastened by strong ropes to trees on the bank, formed a floating dock which rose and fell with the river's whim. In the June floods the water ran brown and swift, and the dock floated but a few feet below the bank's level. With the hot, dry days of August it was necessary to descend roughly hewn steps to a stream that crept sluggishly between sand-bars green with water willows.

On all sides the forest stretched, broken only by water meadows and muskegs feathered with the emerald green of tamarack. Spruce, poplar, birch, and balsam fir formed the main growth; but there are forests within forests, and between the rugged boles of black poplar and blistered trunks of fir there were thickets of mountain maple, hazel, and spotted alder. These formed an undergrowth so dense, so greenly gloomy, and so still, that one had the impression of being in the depths of the sea, and was not surprised by a curiously marine-like growth of ferns and horsetails, through which the tiny wood warblers—mourning, chestnut-sided, and Wilson's—moved like tropical fish.

In this forest any opening, however small—bog, meadow, or old camp site—was as distinctive as is any wooded coulee or poplar bluff on the prairies.

Only from the river was the sky to be seen, and then only by looking upward between the twin leafy walls which rose from the banks like a canyon. All was ordered here, as though arranged with care. First the brownish-grey clay at the muddy water's edge, then the pale emerald of water willow, followed by the yellow-green of Manitoba maple and the pea-green of ash, above which towered the glossy richness of the black poplars and the sombre darkness of spruce, the front ranks of the forest proper.

The clearing had been laboriously hewn out, and it was easy to see that it had to be partly renewed with each season, as the almost tropical growth ever tended to encroach from all sides. Within this open space flowers of every hue rioted, as though conscious of the opportunity to show themselves afforded by the removal of the trees. Wild roses formed a pinkish bank along the river, dandelions speckled with yellow the edges of the faint trail from river to cabin, and wood anemones, delicately white as rice-paper, nodded in the shade. Grasses of a dozen different varieties, ranging from blue-joint to alien timothy brought in with lumbermen's hay, waved their crested heads.

The cabin, of peeled spruce logs with a roof of poles and clay, stood in the centre of the clearing, and the door and window trimmings of white and green betokened that this was no trapper's shack, but a forestry station.

In summer, I know of no place in the West where the bird songs can compare in volume with the moving chorus on Carrot River. There are warblers in hundreds; but these are not sustained singers, and their lisping notes only make an accompaniment to the music of the rose-breasted grosbeaks and the purple finches, and the wonderful song of the hermit thrush. Water thrushes and white-throated sparrows sing constantly, and the tree swallows twitter endlessly. Just as the lakes and ponds of central Saskatchewan are the special kingdom of the water birds and waders, and the sere prairies the domain of the grass sparrows and kindred finches, so is the Carrot River country a most favoured habitat of the more truly woodland species. But this is true only along the river, where the variety of shrubs and trees makes a botanical garden. Back on the pine ridges, in the tamarack swamps, and even more so in the great stretches of spruce forest, bird life is scarce, and the species met with are peculiar to such habitat.

One of the most interesting birds here is the great red-crested pileated woodpecker, that can bore a hole nearly a foot wide and as deep to get spruce-borer larvae from the heart of a tree. Just as the sage grouse epitomizes the dusty cattle country, so does this woodpecker represent, in my mind, the great northern forest.

Travelling in the North can be easy or it can be hard. Travelling down-stream with a good "kicker" (outboard motor) pushing the canoe at a good speed is easy. Working against the current by paddle, with the motor out of action (for one of the many reasons why a motor does go out of action), is heartbreaking.

Winter travel with a good train of dogs following a broken trail, or travelling on the thick smooth ice of a river or lake, can be like a holiday. Breaking trail ahead of the dogs through the deep-drifted snow of a wind-swept muskeg which seems to have no far side is miserable, but no worse than trying to make a patrol in the heavy timber of the hills. There for yards at a time the poor dogs never put foot to ground, but have to climb over a succession of tangled deadfall logs, the legacy of a forest fire or high winds; while the traveller has to heave and haul and push the toboggan to help the dogs. So when people ask, "How far can you go in a day with dogs?" I reply that it all depends. It may be five miles in as many or more hours—sweating, backbreaking hours—or it may be fifty miles, arriving with a merry jingle of dog bells.

It was in order to make patrols in the hills possible that the work of "brushing out"—clearing and blazing narrow trails, no more than footpaths, through these shaggy forests—was undertaken, as well as the putting up of some tiny patrol cabins. These were little more than huts, but still were much better than the open camp where the cold gradually pushed its way into your sleeping-bag while the trees popped explosively with the frost.

These same trails could be used in summer for pack-horses, although their use was limited because in some places there was very little grazing, and the mosquitoes and deer flies bothered them terribly, in spite of all the fly dope that was sprayed on the animals.

From the station, the only view was up and down the river; otherwise, except for the small clearing, all was bush at its nearest, densest and highest, and all beautiful. But the eye wearied of so much beauty of leaf and stem and vine and flower so close at hand, and the time came when I longed to see from a distance, as one who looks at a picture steps back to admire the whole after having taken in the detail.

Then it was a pleasant change to ride to my fire tower on the Jackpine Hill, three miles away on the slope of the Pasquia. There the rich alluvial soil of the river with its luxuriant growth gave way to sandy loam, and scattered jackpines permitted a view of the gentle slope upon which they grew.

In place of ferns, there were thrifty timber grass and chubby little clumps of blueberry bushes, and even a few straggling Saskatoons. But most wonderful of all were the flowers. While the horses grazed (they too appreciated the open space, and kept lifting their heads to gaze around) I wandered far and wide, admiring and happy.

In early May I found prairie crocuses (anemones) there—of all places. They made me think of the far-away prairies from which I was separated by hundreds of miles of solid forest. How they came to be there is a perennial mystery to me. Had they always been there? Had these great hills been once semi-prairie or park-like, as their name would indicate? For Pasquia must surely be an old French way of writing the Cree *puskwa,* and that means prairie. "Puskwa Watchee," Prairie Mountain, the Indians say. And this reminds me that George Simpson relates in his diary (about 1820) that he found Indians hunting buffalo not so far west of here.

Are these then the last surviving plants of a species which has been slowly throttled by the encroaching bush? Or do they owe their being here to some chance seeds brought on the feet of migrating birds? All I know is that here, and nowhere else in the Pasquia, these flowers are found.

In June I was again reminded of the southland by the orange prairie lilies. They were lovely. Patches of violets, too, snuggled down among the short grass, and I could gather great nosegays of them. Mountain ash shrubs seemed to choose this more open and sunny locality to display their coral-like berries; and speaking of berries, this was of course a favourite place to come in August for the purpose of gathering blueberries for pies.

The jackpines themselves were somewhat shaggy old trees, such as are usually found on sand ridges; spaced wide apart and with great twisted overhanging limbs at their crests. It has always seemed to me that the wind rushing through the tops of pine trees makes a sweet sighing sound that one hears among no other trees except their near relatives, the lodge-pole pine. In fact I have often said that if I were taken blindfold and left in a distant forest, I would know whether I was among pine or not by the sound of the wind. And so again there is a reminder of the South; for the wind sighed like this on the lodge-pole-pine slopes of the Cypress Hills years ago.

On Jackpine Hill I listened in vein for the sweet notes of the rose-breasted grosbeak and the water thrush, but I did hear the loud "three beer" cry of the olive-sided flycatcher and was often showered with little scraps sent down by the crossbills that climbed parrot-like among the cones overhead. Pine siskins I also found there, and a pair of clay-coloured sparrows far from their favourite wolf-willow.

At the crest of Jackpine Hill stood the eighty-foot lookout tower, built of spliced jackpine logs and ascended by a rustic ladder.

From the top of the tower I could see away over the low land to the east, where a faint smudge of smoke indicated the great sawmill at The Pas; and between me and it the silvery tracery of the rivers that drain from the hills, the Pasquia and the Waskwie, and their tributary lakes—a network I knew as well as my summer patrol route.

South, the wooded hills stretched on as if for ever, broken only by the great gash which was the Bainbridge Canyon. The western view was the same, while to the north I could see almost to Cumberland Lake.

During December and January the winter evenings began with the lighting of lamps at three in the afternoon; and when not out on patrol I would occupy myself during that time with reports until, those finished and supper eaten, I turned for relaxation to my drawing things. Madeline, the supper dishes washed, would often sit and watch me.

Madeline was a little Saulteaux Indian girl, aged twelve, who could not make a pothook or read a word of either the Cree syllabic or English. Her parents were Christians, and that was why she had a

European name, given at baptism. Her father was my handyman, who fed the sleigh dogs, chopped wood, and tended the horses. He and his wife, with Madeline, occupied a small log cabin to themselves, and his wife used to do my washing, and some cooking, helped by the girl.

One evening Madeline shyly borrowed a pencil, and taking an old piece of departmental stationery which I had spoilt and thrown into the kindling-box, she smoothed it out on the far end of the table and began to draw, her full Indian lips parted and her plaited braids hanging half over her eyes.

I pretended to be absorbed in my own work, and began to wonder what curious thing would come from her pencil. After half an

hour she very quietly laid the paper before me and quickly slipped through the door to her own cabin.

Her half hour's work showed a pair of timber wolves, aroused from sleep among the spruces, looking in the direction of whatever disturbed them. I remembered her father telling me of having seen a pair of wolves like this once, and I remembered also that Madeline had been present while he told it. The sketch is far from highly finished, but it has life, atmosphere, and action. I have kept it carefully for twenty-five years.

Next day Madeline came in early to make tea for me, and I thanked her for the sketch, so that she giggled in embarrassment and pleasure. Thereafter I began to teach her to read and write, and to speak English correctly. She was a good pupil and learned fast; and every available evening we had an hour's lessons, with her dark-faced parents sitting nearby as I required the aid of her father at times to interpret what I wanted to explain to her.

I found out during these lessons why Indians call our beverage cocoa by the curious name of *koko sewin meekoh,* which means pig's blood, and why they shun it as a drink from the association of names.

The first acquaintance the Crees had with pork was during their early contacts with the Hudson's Bay Company, when they were introduced to the salted variety, known as "Hudson Bay salt side." When the Indians asked the French half-breeds what kind of animal this meat came from, they were told its French name, *cochon.* This they soon corrupted to *koko,* so that pork came to be, to them, *koko suweash,* or pig's meat.

The Hudson's Bay did a great trade in tea with the red men, who simply can't do without their *muskeekee apwa,* or medicine drink. But many years later a fur trader obtained a bulk lot of cheap cocoa and tried to introduce the Indians to it. Had it borne another name he might have been successful; but when the Indians asked the name, and then looked at it and tried a little on the finger, they came to the conclusion that it was dried pig's blood, and it bears that name among them to this day.

Before a year was out, Madeline's parents wished to return to their reserve far away, and I have not seen the girl since. I hope she got the chance of more schooling, and I hope she developed that natural talent for drawing which so many Indian children have.

CHAPTER SEVENTEEN

Unexpected Meetings

WE MAY spend much time in well-planned attempts to study more closely some of the intimate habits of the wild things, only to find ourselves, all too often, frustrated by wind or weather, or by the absence from their usual haunts of the creatures we desire to see. All the more memorable, therefore, are the unexpected meetings which so often brighten our wanderings along the woodland trails.

Such an event occurred while I was mushing along a trail which paralleled the Carrot River and was separated from it only by a narrow fringe of bush, which at places contained so meagre a growth that I had an almost unobstructed view of the frozen channel. The month was February. Although the snow was deep the weather was not intensely cold, and bright sunshine fell through the branches and enlivened the drifted snow on the river. For days we had heard timber wolves howling and had seen many tracks; but Lupus is one of the shyest of creatures and has such fear of man as to make him one of the rarest animals to see.

Jogging along behind the dogs, I was in the habit of constantly watching the river. There seemed to be a fascination in seeing its curves straighten out as we came abreast. It must be explained that the well-trodden trail was much lower than the snow and small bush on either side, therefore the dogs' vision was limited strictly to what lay straight ahead and they could not see the river.

Rounding a bend, I could see something dark on the river about a quarter of a mile ahead, and as we came closer I looked for an opening through which I could get a better view, thinking at first that it

170

might be a deer lying wounded, for whatever it was seemed to be close to the snow except for what might be its head. For a few hundred yards the bush on the riverside was very dense, but soon thinned out and promised to give me the desired view. Stopping the dogs, who neither saw, heard, nor smelt anything out of the way, I stepped off the trail so as to look down on the river. And there, only a few rods from me and separated by not so much as a tree, sat a splendid wolf.

He was twice as large as any of my huskies, with a fine brush. He sat as a dog sits, on his haunches, with front paws together and tail curled around. From between his erect ears sprang the first coarse hairs of his grizzled mane. His yellow eyes looked straight up at me, with neither fear nor anger in their depth. So I have seen a dog look. And, like a dog, he dropped his eyes presently and half lifted one paw as if uneasy. Having satisfied my curiosity I picked up my toboggan rope, spoke quietly to the dogs and continued my journey.

I think he was simply sunning himself after a full meal, and I believe he was so well fed that his senses were dulled, and that because of our relative positions and the direction of the wind he neither smelt nor heard me. See me he undoubtedly did; but he certainly did not recognize me for what I was.

Another time I was riding horseback along a bush road that was pretty well grown up in long grass, when from just ahead around a bend, I heard a most peculiar whimpering, crying sound intermingled with growls. Touching my horse, I rounded the bend and there pulled up short to see what was almost under foot. Two animals fighting it appeared to be, one red, one greyish.

Over and over they went, paying no attention to me or my horse; but so rapidly did they move and so long and tangled was the herbage that for the life of me I could not get a proper view. I therefore dismounted, thinking that it was a very large pine marten attacking a groundhog.

Just as I was about to enter the fray with a stick, the reddish one saw me and sprang away in fear, followed by the other still growling at her heels and biting at her tail, till a more sudden and frightened move on her part caused him, too, to turn and regard me. Immediately his demeanour also changed and he followed, slinking behind her like a schoolboy caught at the jam pot.

They were foxes—she a handsome red vixen, thin from nursing, and appearing lither than a fox should; he her own pup, about two months old. They had been playing in sheer joy to the abandonment of their usual wariness, even to not heeding the thudding of my horse's hooves so close, and as a result had been caught in the act very nicely.

The wind on this occasion too was in my favour, which strengthens my belief that many wild animals are scarcely sensitive to danger unless their noses carry the message. I suppose the foxes had often been approached by moose, whose heavy bodies would jar the ground just as much as my horse did.

Another incident occurred while I was surveying a trail in the forest. I had gone ahead of my companions on snowshoes, facing a medium wind with light snow. Coming to an open burned area, I espied a fine cow moose with her calf, browsing contentedly on the twigs of second-growth white poplar that protruded a few feet above the deep snow. She was right in my line of travel, and I continued straight towards her till I was within twenty feet.

Something told me that if she raised her head and turned she might be cross, so to warn her I spoke. "Come on, old lady, I want to pass." The calf turned his head, stared at me like a domestic cow's calf, and went on eating. I spoke again. The cow slowly turned and on seeing me, swung her hind parts around so as to be sideways to me. I carried a hatchet in my belt, and taking it from its loop I chucked it underhand at her so as to strike her on the flank. She moved away at a walk, followed by her calf. I went forward and swung around on the other side of her. That gave her my scent and she departed in a great hurry, running with that smart high-kneed Hackney trot which moose use to such advantage among tangled deadfall.

Moving silently on my snowshoes, I had made no sound to disturb her; and until she got my scent, no voice of instinct spoke to her. This was in a great wilderness where not even Indians penetrated, and I doubt if she had ever seen a man before.

Once in the Niska Creek country I nearly fell over two very young moose calves. They are so like reddish-brown foals that I don't think you would notice the difference if you saw one in the home pasture. The ears are a little larger, it is true, but the shape of the head is very like, as the long rounded lip which the moose finds so useful for browsing—for they do not graze—has not yet developed.

I stood looking down at these fine youngsters for a moment or so, but neither saw nor heard the mother. They lay motionless till I quietly turned to leave them, when one stumbled to its feet, and uttering a soft bleat came toward me. I tried to push it away or frighten it, but nothing doing—it followed me bleating to the creek bank fifty yards away, where I took to my canoe and left it.

I expect the mother located it without any trouble; but half the settlers who raise fawns and moose calves probably pick them up on occasions like that, in the quite honest belief that they have been abandoned. The moose mother might have been far away feeding, trusting to her youngsters to lie perfectly still while she was gone. Range cows similarly leave their calves and feed perhaps a mile away; but it doesn't do to jump to the conclusion that these mothers abandon their young.

Twice I have seen deer beset by wolves. Once a white-tailed doe was chased into my yard in the North by timber wolves, and once I saw a black-tailed buck pulled down by coyotes in the Cypress Hills.

In the first case it was January. I was just feeding my sleigh dogs when my attention was attracted by a curious roaring noise, and presently the doe came in view. She was so nearly played out that she was staggering and barely able to step over the fallen logs. She came straight on, my huskies almost going mad with excitement. She detoured a little to avoid coming too close to the kennels, and then I heard the moaning howl of one wolf, and then another. My dogs answered in that blood-curdling howl which is peculiarly their own. The doe never stopped till she came to the hay corral behind my barn, and then she stood still, her tongue sticking straight out like an exhausted cattle beast, and still breathing through her mouth with a roar which threatened to burst her lungs. She stayed around two days before she departed, quite herself again.

On the other occasion it was also winter and I was riding over the bench when I came to a trampled spot in the snow, with some small bloodstains. More tracks led on, then there was another trampled spot and more bloodstains. As I came round the shoulder of the hill I saw the end, and did not interfere as I knew I was too late.

Two coyotes had a great buck at bay, with his back to a willow bush. One coyote lay on his belly behind the buck, the other circled and feinted at the animal's throat. Each time he did this the buck took a step or two forward with his antlers down, and then the coyote behind him would take advantage of this and rush in from behind to nip at his legs. The buck was practically hamstrung when I came in view and in a few moments all was over. It was a sad sight, but a most interesting one for a naturalist.

Much happier was our prolonged encounter with our Waskwei moose. We first saw him one September morning as we followed the narrow pack trail which we had cut out and blazed the previous winter, leading south across the White Poplar and the Thickbush to the Waskwei, and thence across the hills to Otosquen.

This trail crosses through the very heart of the Pasquia Hills, through country never now penetrated by either white man or red, although at one time no doubt the Indians sometimes got that far when hunting. It is a country of such heavy bush and such immense trees that it is almost impossible to get any kind of view, except sometimes by climbing a tree on a high point. In summer the woods are so thickly leafed that it is almost a jungle; in winter they are sombre and dark, lonely and somewhat forbidding, especially to one who, like myself, has spent so many years on the plains with nothing between the sun and the earth.

In autumn or Indian summer they are at their best. The days are warm and mellow, with perhaps a slight frost at night. The twigs of the deciduous trees are becoming bare, helping to let the sun in. What leaves remain have turned to bright yellow and orange, so that the contrast with the dark spruce is most delightful; and the great birches in particular show off better then than at any other season. The soft smell of autumn and the absence of mosquitoes add to the attractions.

My patrolman, a splendid young Swede, first noticed the moose as we coaxed the brown pack-mare down the steep bank of Thickbush Creek. The animal, a young bull, was coming towards us up the creek bank with that disregard for caution and that cowed demeanour which meant only one thing—that he had challenged and been whipped by an older bull, and was heading for other parts as fast as his aching legs could carry him. His breathing was laboured and gait stumbling, and he came within fifty yards before he saw us, as we stood tightening the lash rope over the pack which the mare carried. He paused, stood for a moment looking quite helpless, and then sneaked off into the bush.

The load was awkward and heavy, containing not only grub and blankets, but an axe and a crosscut saw for felling trees and a single set of harness for hauling logs, besides sundry other tools and a small crated window, for we were on our way to put up a patrol cabin on the Waskwei River. It was some time before we had adjusted this pack, which had slipped somewhat in crossing the creek;

and by the time we had done so, the moose was forgotten. However, later in the afternoon the mare looked back over her shoulder several times, and Gus finally said he thought something was following us.

We reached the Waskwei that night and made camp. Jill, the mare, we put on picket among the pea vine until bedtime. Then we brought her to camp, tied her up, and gave her a small feed of oats, for we did not want her stampeded in the darkness by bears. During the night we heard some breaking of twigs, and once the mare whinnied, but that was nothing unusual and did not disturb us.

In the morning, while Gus made a bannock, I took a pail and went down to the creek for water. Seeing a moose track crossing the creek, I back-tracked it from curiosity and found that the animal had come over our trail the night before. After circling the camp, it had departed across the creek, swinging west up the south bank towards the higher ground beyond, which was slightly more open and covered very thickly with wiry hazel bush, among which dead tree trunks made a hideous tangle.

Returning to camp I told Gus, and we both felt that this might be the moose we had seen. The high birch and spruce hills bordering the Waskwei are not a favoured moose range at this time of the year. The animals much prefer the semi-open meadows of the low land to the east, to which the Thickbush and Waskwei flow; and in that part moose tracks are so common everywhere that we wouldn't even have remarked on one.

The next couple of days were spent felling trees and sawing them into logs. During that time we saw no moose, but twice or thrice heard a rather half-hearted moose call from up the creek, and knew that the animal was still about, in spite of our talking and the noise of our work.

Jill gave us very little trouble, for she was an old bush horse and quite accustomed to camp life, although she simply couldn't help getting her picket rope tangled several times a day, as there was really no such thing as any open grazing, and she had to pick about in the smaller bush. On the third day we hitched her up and commenced hauling the logs into a square for building.

About three o'clock in the afternoon, with the westering sun beating hotly on us, I was just taking the log chain from the butt of a spruce when the mare gave a snort and looked up the creek bank; and then she jumped forward, all but catching my hand in the chain.

I called "Whoa!" and grabbing her dangling halter shank, looked in the same direction.

With a crash of brush a bull moose came into view, his head high, his antlers laid well back over his humping shoulders, in the high-kneed trotting strides of his kind. He charged directly towards us, and Gus grabbed for his rifle. Although this was a game reserve, and we of all men should be the first to observe the no-hunting rule, we always had arms for an emergency; and this seemed about to be one, for an angry bull moose is a most unpleasant customer.

At the same time I shouted "Hi!" and the bull stopped dead, his legs sprawled out, his head down, and all the bristles along his hump standing on end.

"Hold on, Gus," I shouted. "I don't think he'll come any closer." And he didn't; after standing there surveying us for perhaps a minute, he slipped away in that perfectly quiet way of a moose that does not wish to be seen. The mare seemed to have recovered from her fear —she must have seen dozens of moose in her day—and we resumed our work.

Thereafter, we heard the moose call every night, and the funny thing was that Jill often whinnied in reply; and regularly every afternoon for the week more that we camped there, the young bull—for according to his antlers he was only three or four years old—charged crashing down the creek bank to within about a hundred yards, where he would survey the camp, and then silently steal away.

We got to expect him, and so did the brown mare, who pricked her ears towards the west when she knew he was coming; while the squirrel which had adopted us and our camp, chattered from his perch on the partly finished cabin.

There is no doubt that this moose, defeated in his fight with the larger bull, dared not venture again that fall into the domain of his rival, but for some curious reason had followed us to the Waskwei. As the rut worked him up, he became interested in our brown mare, so like a moose in colour and general shape; and yet she puzzled him. She on her part felt friendly, as horses are very gregarious and hate being alone. Deer, similarly, often pal up with milch cows in a bush pasture; and for all I know Jill may have had a moose friend or two when, as a filly, she ran in the woods of Kamsack.

When the cabin was finished, complete with window and rough-hewn door, we left the Waskwei; and I did not revisit the cabin till the first snowfall took me there on patrol with toboggan and dogs.

My little squirrel chattered at me from the spruce by the cabin, but I saw no moose or any track of his kind.

Then there was the time I came to one of my far patrol cabins as dusk was falling. Cold and tired, I left the dogs lying in harness while I entered the small moss-chinked building to start a fire. After the snowy outdoors, the far corners of the cabin seemed gloomy, but at the head of my fern-cushioned bunk I could see something long and dark with bright eyes. Realizing it was some animal I hastily shut the door behind me, and groping in my parka, found a match and lit the candle stump on the low shelf by the door.

As I did so the creature, which in the glow of the match looked as big as a lynx, leaped to the sandy floor and then into the big tin stove through one of the kettle holes from which the lid was already dislodged. Then a great commotion took place as the animal tried to scramble up the inside of the five-inch stovepipe. It would apparently get up part way, only to fall back in a cloud of ashes. I realized that this was the road by which the creature had entered the cabin, and knew it could be no animal as big as a lynx.

I therefore opened the door and stepped back to give the creature a chance to show itself and escape. Presently a narrow head with bright eyes and short ears, poised on a small neck, peered forth, only to be quickly withdrawn again. I stood perfectly still. In a few moments the movement was repeated, and, apparently satisfied that here was no trap but a chance to leap for liberty, the animal shot its whole beautiful body forth in a great leap, landing with all four feet together on the doorsill, and thence went in great curving bounds through the snowy woods. It was one of the loveliest and rarest of fur-bearers—a pekan or fisher.

A tour of inspection around the cabin told the whole story. The fisher had been squirrelling, and followed one of the little chatterers down the stovepipe, killing it in the stove as the remains showed. Thereafter it had found itself trapped and had made itself very much at home, eating my bacon and other provisions and curling up at sleeping time in the lair it had hollowed out among the soft ferns of the bunk.

Needless to say, the squirrel had been visiting the empty shack for some time, as my store of prunes and beans bore witness.

Of all Canadian birds none bear so appropriate a name as the snowflakes or snowbirds, small buntings that come to us from the Northland, bringing with them the very spirit of Canadian winters.

It seems to me that our interest in native birds hangs more upon association than upon actual knowledge or direct contact with them. For instance, it is the rich notes of a robin heralding spring that endear him to us. His voice fills us with memories—the smell of warming sod, the rare perfume of bursting tree buds. His song means more than his red breast. The bright bluebird flashing by carries our fancy back to disturbing winds that last March filled us with poetic longings. The sound of vireos warbling like a cool brook through July heat takes us back to early summer mornings in the garden.

It is thus the snowflakes have endeared themselves to the Canadian people. They sweep down from the Arctic with winter's first blast, great flocks of them—staunch, vivacious sprites, dancing before vicious winds, chanting sweet notes through howling gales. Alive they are to the challenge of a cruel season, fearless as the trapper who goes into the blizzard, sturdy as the farmer who battles the frost, cheerful as the cowhand who whistles through the drifts.

It is thus I shall always remember them; and not only as harbingers of winter elements, but themselves a feathered tempest as they gather in vast flocks and roll like white clouds over the fields, forging on and on in front of the wind.

I shall never forget one ride I had through a storm of snowflakes. This was not the first time I had seen flocks of breathless magnitude, but never before had I experienced the exhilaration of being lost in a blizzard of living, breathing, singing birds.

Riding one day late in April over the meadow road west of The Pas, in northern Manitoba, I was delighted by the sight of a storm of snowbirds of such magnitude that I could well have believed that I really was in the midst of a belated blizzard. It had rained a little the night before and then frozen, so that the road and the cultivated ground resembled dark metal. Starting about half a mile ahead of me, the road was completely white for at least another half mile, and so were the fields for as great a distance on either side.

As I rode nearer, the snowfield turned to a blizzard of flying snowbirds. They rose from the ground with a swish of tiny wings, like real snowflakes whirled upwards by the wind. They blocked the very light of the sun and left me in a storm-like gloom. They seemed all around—below, under my horse's feet and belly, on all sides, and above. Several brushed softly against my hat, and I instinctively put a hand over my mouth and nose as one does in a storm.

My horse Jack snorted and shied and struck with his front hooves. Willow bushes, relieved of their load, sprang sharply upward into shape; but before their branches had stilled, they were again loaded down. As though storm-tossed, these lovely snowflakes passed over and around me. Battalions would alight on the road ahead for a bare second, then they were tossed upward, snatched backward, and dropped gently to earth behind me, while others took their place in front. And all the time smaller flocks within the greater passed and repassed, swerving to avoid collision; and indeed, the great wonder to me was that with all this apparently involuntary action, no accident befell these animated snowflakes.

Snow buntings they are named by naturalists, but the country people call them snowbirds or snowflakes, these small finches, about the size of a house sparrow. It is when seen in the spring after winter's grip has left the land that they most resemble snowflakes, because then they are much whiter than in the fall, and the dapper, immaculate creatures show little or no trace of the rusty overwash which was so noticeable before Christmas.

This change in dress is not due to a process of moulting, which would certainly be hard on such small creatures during the cold months, but to a wearing down of the rusty edges of the feathers so that only the pure white is left. The wings and tail show pure black instead of rusty black, also because of the wearing down of the feathers. All dressed up in their new spring outfits, the birds gather in greater flocks than ever, ready for the long journey to their breeding-grounds.

If we were to follow them, what a vast and complete view of an unknown Canada would meet our eyes! For their happy journey carries them over the great evergreen forests north of the Saskatchewan River, past Reindeer Lake, the meeting-ground of the Cree and Chipwyan Indians, past the last frontiers of settled population, to a bleak wilderness of muskeg and rock and lake and uncharted stream. The Barren Lands, it is commonly called; but Stefansson, that great Canadian explorer, used a more apt and poetic name—the Arctic Prairies.

Here for a few brief months, nodding grasses and low-nestled flowers mark a hurried summer. And our little birds spread far and wide over these prairies. They cross the wide stretches of salt water that divide the mainland from the arctic islands, within nodding distance of the Pole. Here on these Arctic Prairies, a bright picture comes to mind when we think of the snowflakes—white birds skimming like fairies over carpets of dancing flowers; white birds chanting sweet notes into the rushing winds, sweeping over cool pools and soggy marshes where the blue sky is caught in sudden snatches. Here they share their days with the watchful snowy owl, and with the mottled ptarmigans who call to each other from knoll to knoll.

A quiet, peaceful scene, and well suited to the snowflakes for making love and building nests, and breeding new flocks. Not that enemies are absent, for the arctic fox hunts them with great cunning, the hovering falcon strikes down on them with deadly talon, and some fall victim to the blunt wooden arrows of the Eskimo children who shoot gleefully at the small white birds, carrying them home in triumph to be plucked and spitted for dinner.

Strangely, the snowflakes do not choose to winter in the shelter of the forests, but spread over the prairies, often in company with redpolls, sometimes even being joined by the grey-crowned rosy finches from the mountains. Here is the same generally level and monotonous landscape as on the tundras, broken only occasionally by low ranges of hills. The same wind constantly flattens the herbage and there is the same absence of trees or bold landmarks.

The effect of man's penetration and settlement of the prairies has been a boon to the snowflakes, for wherever man has tilled the soil and constructed roads, there have sprung up weeds; and these weeds, protruding from the snow, bear on their dead stalks the food which means life to these feathered folk. The flocks feed busily to the accompaniment of much subdued twittering as they follow a fence row or a roadside. There is a never-ending game of leap-frog going on as the rearmost birds fly jerkily to the front of the flock, only to find themselves, in a short space of time, once more the last stragglers.

And so they put in the winter, small flocks and large flocks, here today and gone tomorrow as the exigencies of food conditions and weather take them. For days they may be gone, and then suddenly they throng our barnyards, or even our city blocks. We, tied to our daily tasks, hardly notice them, except when on the lonely trails we are reminded of them as their gentle notes drift down to us from the wintry sky. Waiting for a midnight bus on King Street in Regina, I once heard these same notes, coming from the air far above the sound of motor traffic.

It is during their winter roamings, as they brush amongst the brittle weeds and low shrubbery, that the rusty overwash on their feathers wears off. With the partial thaws of March, the purity of their whiteness, as well as the brighter and longer days, makes us realize their presence.

But on this rare April day when I rode spellbound into a storm of migrating snowflakes, the ground was black from the thaw and contrasted vividly with their immaculate plumage. As I passed through the flock, the birds' twittering rose and fell in sweet tinkling accompaniment to their soft movement. And I found my thoughts going with this merry throng, going north, back over the forests to their arctic summerland, over the still-frozen lakes and through the winds. I thought that here at last was the real and wonderful Spring Ballet, performed by migrating flocks of humble little birds, not for applause or admiration, but simply as an expression of their everlasting faith in the miracle of the seasons, the miracle of the coming of spring in their vast land of safety and beauty and richness.

Such were my thoughts as I travelled through this wonderful snow-storm. It was fully an hour before their ranks began to thin, for the storm seemed to have followed me. But gradually the last were left behind.

I turned in the saddle that I might see their white beauty and hear the last echoes of their gentle notes, and as I coaxed my horse to a trot I knew that the day had been made unforgettable.

And so one never knows what the day may bring forth to those who travel the woodlands where man is the intruder.

CHAPTER EIGHTEEN

Logs and Cranes

IN MAY the great river flows full from bank to bank, swollen by the winter's snows.

The water is brown and muddy and the current is swift, forever cutting away portions of bank that fall with a sullen splash into the moving tide. For days now we have been waiting for the logs to come down. Each spring the great spruce logs cut by the company fifty miles up-river pass my station on the way to the distant city where the mill's hungry saws await them.

Already the jam crews have established their camps at strategic places along the bank, and they too await the logs with peevies and cant hooks. Their job is to keep an eye on them as they pass, patrolling the riverside wherever there is danger of logs catching on the bank and so drifting sideways to hold up oncoming logs, thus starting a jam which will hold back the whole lot and may cause injury or even death to those who must break it.

The amount of work they will have to do depends to a great extent on how well the work of cleaning up the banks was done last winter by the crew of Indians which the company engaged for the purpose. This work consists of chopping away any trees that have fallen into the river's edge or which project from the bank as the result of a landslide or high winds. To clean up thus a hundred-odd miles of winding river bank is no small task, but it must be done every year.

These lumberjacks now reclining on the river banks were brought up by the barge, a great scow-like affair with quarters roofed in for eating and sleeping; and it in turn was towed up-river by a powerful little inboard motor boat. It has dropped men off at intervals all the way from The Pas, and the last men with their cook will form the nucleus of the "rearing" crew—that is, the crew which will bring up the rear of the drive, taking care to roll into the water any logs left stranded on the banks, for "the flood" does not last long, and the river may start to drop before the logs get down.

The work of putting the logs into the river has already been accomplished by the crew at the landing camp, which is a camp established at a point on the river as near as possible to where the logs are being cut in the hills by the men of the logging camps. From the logging camps they are hauled to the landings by tractors in great trains of as many as twenty sleds. These landings are strips along the river bank from which all trees and stumps have been removed, so that logs can be unloaded and put into the river with not so much as a rose brier to obstruct the work. They are usually about half to three-quarters of a mile long and three hundred yards wide, so that it will be seen that there is work for a fair crew of men on this job alone; and since the camps move to new locations almost each season, new landings also have to be constantly made.

The day comes when we get word from one of the men up-river: "The logs are coming." Before long we can hear them—no loud noise, but more of a murmur made up of the sound of log bumping gently on log in constant repetition, for this is not a fast river as rivers go, and she is gentle with her burden.

And now we see them rounding the bend, sepia and chestnut and Vandyke brown in the sunlight, purplish or bluish-grey in the bank's shade, with square-cut ends of clearest gold. Some are shaggy old veterans and some smooth-barked striplings, but most are even-barked trees in their prime. Here one, jostled by its neighbour as they pass us, executes a complete reversal of ends—slowly, very slowly, while we wonder if it is going to start a jam. But no, it in turn nudges its neighbour, which gives way, and that one the next, until the whole river from bank to bank mutters its resentment at the rudeness.

The first crowded lot goes slowly by and then they come for a while only in twos and threes and odd dozens; but this thin company again gives way to a more impatient throng and the jostling recommences. It reminds us of the way a herd of cattle will have their peaceful progress disturbed by one ill-natured beast which bunts its neighbour, which bunts *its* neighbour, and so on till all the herd is bunting with a dull click of horns.

Towards evening we notice the logs are travelling more slowly and crowding one another, till the whole river is solid logs of every hue of brown, and many are dark and shining from having been submerged from time to time by their comrades. Gradually all motion ceases and a vast dull grinding and groaning is heard as the steady procession from up-stream pushes against the vanguard. There is a jam down below Blackie's camp, and all night the lumberjacks work. By morning the logs are moving freely again. And so for a week this strange slow procession passes.

Great trees that grew for years in the wilderness may have seemed safe from the woodsman; but the timber cruisers penetrate the deepest forests, and for years men have been waiting for the day when they would start to cut down these smooth trunks which will no more be shelter for the chattering squirrels or hunting-grounds for the keen-eyed martens, but will stand again to protect their takers from cold and rain and wind.

Slowly and in stately manner the great scow of the "rearing" crew rounds the bend. Smoke comes from the kitchen amidships and washing flutters on the line. As dark falls she is moored to the bank while the hungry crew clamber on board for the evening meal and their short recreation before they throw themselves into their bunks.

Slowly the moon comes up from behind the dark spruce. Amid the hum of conversation a fiddle-string twangs. "Come on, Frenchy," we hear. A voice singing "A la claire fontaine." Clapping. Then "En roulent ma boule" and the whole crew joining in with a roar. Thumping of feet to "Turkey in the Straw." One last song, "The Curse of Michigan." The light in the floating bunkhouse snaps out.

With the first light the scow comes to life again; mooring-ropes are coiled and slowly she moves down-stream.

As the voices become lost around the bend, the river is left strangely tranquil, and strangely lonely, its annual service to man accomplished.

The first week of June had already passed when we started out for Niska Lake in the hope of finding nesting cranes. Therefore we hardly expected to see eggs, but hoped we might locate the young. There was always the possibility, though, that incubation might not be over for all the birds, since our earlier observations led us to expect several pairs of them.

About the end of April we had been camped on the Niska Creek —of which the lake is simply a marshy widening—and had been thrilled by a close-up view of the cranes' spring dance. We had been paddling along the grassy bank in the cool, pearly dawn, on the lookout for birds, when we heard the unmistakable grating cry of cranes. Peering through the bleached tussocks, we saw the birds, fourteen or fifteen in number—solemnly saluting each other, pairing off with deep bows, and bending their long necks with a serpentine movement.

Every now and again the courtly motions were exchanged for ludicrous buffoonery, as the birds leaped into the air with their wide wings flapping and legs kicking. The clown-like effect was enhanced by the mist, which seemed to both enlarge and distort their forms, and in which at times they seemed to swim.

Sometimes an amorous swain would bend low, low, until the bill, head and very neck lay flat on the ground. Then slowly and with sinuous movement he would raise first the bill, up-pointed to the sky, then the head, and finally the neck, which would then be curved backward till the head rested between the bases of the wings, with the beak pointed still to the sky. In this posture he would commence to pace in a circle, lifting his feet like a Hackney. In the midst of this solemn parade one or another would suddenly clap his wings and commence the ridiculous jumping.

For upward of an hour we watched them till with the mounting sun they became hungry and gradually drifted away from the dancing-spot and commenced to feed, still in pairs.

It was in the hope—indeed the expectation—that these same birds had stayed at Niska Lake to nest, that we made our second trip. True, flocks of little brown cranes had but recently been passing overhead bound for the northern tundras; but our birds were true sand-hill cranes, almost as big as the whooping cranes, than which no North American bird is larger. Having seen the stately wild turkeys leave the cultivated and (at the time of writing) drouth-stricken prairies, we realized that the day might not be far when the sand-hill crane would be a bird only to be seen in museums.

We thought that if they nested anywhere in Northern Saskatchewan, Niska Lake might be that place, remote as it is from civilization. It lies within the boundaries of the Pasquia Provincial Forest— forty-odd townships of hill and plain, bushy muskeg and meadow, untracked and uninhabited save by the moose and the fox and the other furred and feathered inhabitants of the North.

Since we should find water too shallow for a motor, we chose a light canoe with a view to the swampy portages. Having packed blankets, grub and other necessities into it, we started down the Carrot River from the Mountain Cabin ranger station on the first lap of a journey which was to be of the most exhausting nature, despite its distance of barely twenty miles. Six miles from the starting-point, we left the river and cooked dinner. Then we had to portage into a smallish muskeg lake called Helldiver.

This portage was one and a half miles long, but by the time we had made two trips apiece we thought it had been ten. The mosquitoes hummed in a vicious cloud and the bulldog flies lived up to their name. The portage was only a roughly cut trail, four feet wide, through tamarack swamp where water lay up to a foot deep, and tangled roots and insecure grass tussocks vied with deep quagmirish holes to ensnare our feet. The sun beat hot and fierce and the stagnant water gave off sickly humid vapours, so that one felt a weakness that was not all born of the strain of heavy packsacks or the bite of the tumpline, and a languidness that even the ever present irritation of the humming insects and the painful wounds which they inflicted could not dispel.

But he who wishes to see wild things must go to them on their terms, and wretched as we were we had the pleasure of hearing and seeing yellow throats (they had not been observed at Mountain Cabin) and redstarts, and we stumbled upon a swamp sparrow's nest in a tuft of rank grass in the middle of the portage.

The worst part of all was the approach to and the margin of the lake itself, which was simply floating bog, so soft that a tussock stepped upon sank a foot or more into the underlying water, but would very slowly rise to the surface again after the weight was removed. So, fighting insects, dripping sweat, stumbling and sometimes falling in the mire or trapped by hidden roots, we finally launched our canoe in Helldiver and got our stuff stowed. Paddling down the lake seemed like heaven, although in spots the water was so shallow that we had to pole the canoe through a rank growth of horsetails and water arrowhead. The wild callas were almost ready to open and we saw where moose had been pulling up and eating the roots.

The eastern shore of the lake was no dryer than any other spot, but a clump of dark spruce and a few birches looked nice and offered a change from the too vivid green of the larch tamarack. Landing near there, we portaged into Loon Lake, a very similar body of water. All that has been said of the first portage would apply— only, as my companion said, double; but we were weary, and in truth this portage was much shorter. These portages, by the way, had been roughly traced by Indians from The Pas who had been wont to poach muskrats. The Rangers had put a stop to *that*, but we were glad to use the old portages.

Crossing Loon Lake we observed most of the common ducks, and in addition a pair of fat, complacent scoters (white winged) and some ruddy ducks, the males' white cheeks very prominent. Black terns "peeked" all around us. Holbœll's and pied-billed grebes were beginning to be noisy, for by now the sun's rays came slantingly through the conifers of the shore-line. We located and headed towards the lobstick which marked the portage into Shorson Creek.

(In making a lobstick a tall, and if possible lone, spruce is chosen. It is climbed and with a hand axe the limbs just below the top are lopped (lobbed) for ten or twelve feet downward, leaving an area of naked trunk surmounted by a feathery top. Such a mark can be picked out easily, either in summer or when after freeze-up the canoe routes are followed by dog trains. Lobsticks are the road markers of the North.)

This one was on a dry timber ridge separating us from the Shallow and Niska Lakes meadow country; and as dusk was falling, we camped at its base that night. We slept well, for we had a mosquito net. Our bacon sizzled early the next morning, and the sun was still low when we nosed the canoe through the tall reeds into the creek— named for my patrolman the previous year, for this was unsurveyed country and only the larger waters had names.

Small as the creek was—barely eight feet wide—the current was swift, for it bore hill water to these lowlands; and, with only occasional pushes from the paddle to nose our craft around the many sharp twists and turns, we were borne onward. The margin was walled by tall reeds, back of which were semi-open hay meadows studded with clumps of willow in resemblance of a park. What a relief to be out of the stifling bush-muskeg, we said; and then through an opening in the reeds we saw the hills from whence we had come, lying calm and blue with little fleecy clouds hanging on their crests. The west wind swept from their timbered heights and over the grasslands to refresh our bodies and heal our bites.

The country hereabouts seemed to lose its harsh northern aspect and reminded us of the western prairies we had known, especially the hay flats around Jackfish Lake in the old settled Battleford district. We began to see the birds typical of such a habitat, too, and noted Savannah, Nelson, and Laconte sparrows in the grass. Red-winged blackbirds and bronzed grackles nested in the bordering reeds, but we looked in vain this day for the yellow-headed member of this garrulous fraternity. A colony of short-billed marsh wrens were picked out by their note from the meadows, and long-billed wrens scuttled and scolded fearlessly in the reeds. A marsh hawk floated overhead.

As we entered Shallow Lake, into which this creek discharges, I remarked that this looked like phalerope country, although I had not yet seen one in the district. Sure enough, within a few minutes we observed several of these beautiful birds puddling about in the oozy margin, the females gay with shiny chestnut side-necks, the subdued-looking males sober in grey.

Sora rails could be heard frequently, and once or twice the unmistakable grating note of the Virginia rail. I have never heard the yellow rail here in north-eastern Saskatchewan, although I found them not uncommon north of Battleford and along the western border of the province. My companion produced a pocket comb, scratching which with a fingernail produced a sound sufficiently resembling the Virginia rail's call to bring one bird quite close. Only the answering call and slight movement in the rushes indicated his location, as these are among the most exasperatingly difficult birds to flush, or even to see.

As the creek had plenty of water to float a canoe, we had hoped that Shallow Lake might belie its name and be of a paddling depth; but alas, it was so extremely shallow that for the first two miles of its three-mile length the canoe dragged on the mud and we were forced to get out and haul it along with a rope. The bottom being soft mud into which one sank over the knees made this exhausting work; but, as a compensation, the breeze continued and we were free from mosquitoes. Hard as it was, this dragging business was better than attempting to carry the canoe and equipment around the grassy and bushy shore.

On the farther shore two cow moose with calves at foot rooted among the lily pads. We had spent so much time on the way, and the going was so laboriously slow, that it was dinner-time when we reached the far end of the lake and, with the current in our favour, paddled into Waskwei (Birch-bark) River. Down this we had to paddle five miles, between lovely grassy banks which in places gave way to woods wherein spruce mingled with poplar, maple, and ash to form a mosaic of soft greens banked by wild roses.

Widgeon and teal constantly rose before us with soft whistles, always dropping around the next bend into the clear stream and rising again as we came into view. A family party of otters were playing tag around an old willow root, but on sighting us they dived headfirst from the bank like so many seals and were not seen again.

Rounding one sharp bend, we met a cow moose with twin calves almost head-on. The water was only about three feet deep, and came only up to her knees, while the youngsters—whom she must have led into the water to rid them of flies—showed only their heads and a strip of chocolate-coloured back. All three faced us and stared, with their large ears up, mule-like. The canoe drifted to within twelve feet of them. I remembered that any wild mother is to be respected, and had no wish to see our light craft crushed by her sharp hooves; so I rather hurriedly waved a paddle and shouted. Thereat she turned and lunged up the clay bank, followed by the calves, who turned perfectly together like a matched team, and kept side by side up the incline and out of sight.

So we paddled in the afternoon sun, the pied water dancing before us, till we reached the mouth of Niska Creek. This stream is tributary to the Waskwei, so we found its current against us. Only two miles up its green and limpid waters we came to extensive hay meadows margining the lake, and a delightful sight they were, decked with round willow clumps beyond which a line of dark spruce marked the base of the blue hills.

Our hopes seemed about to be fulfilled, for at this moment we heard the calls of cranes, but at some little distance. As it was supper-time, my companion suggested making camp in a spruce grove on what we named Rocky Point. We decided to leave bird-hunting for the morrow. I wanted to make a sketch of the point—the dark spruce rising to the sky from a base of tender-green, soft willows, all reflected so perfectly that one was at a loss to know where land and water met.

Unfortunately the wind had dropped with the sun, and the mosquitoes rose in such angry swarms that today when I look at that sketch I involuntarily scratch my bites. As I worked, a party of yellow-legs came piping overhead and, describing a sudden half-circle, alighted at the water's edge within a few feet of me. They were accompanied by several rather chunkier, darker birds. I had to look twice before I identified the latter as ruddy-breasted long-billed dowitchers—not breeding, I thought; and this assumption was proved correct when a specimen was taken the next day. Their softer yelping mingled harmoniously with the flute-like notes of their yellow-legged companions. These birds were presently joined by several female phaleropes (Wilson's), grunting softly.

As I dropped to sleep that night, the Wilson's snipe drummed overhead and bitterns primed their pumps.

The whitethroats, pileated woodpeckers and Canada jays typical of the northern woods (Hudsonian Zone) seemed very far away in this transplanted island of Transition Zone. Nevertheless, the first song to greet us at dawn was the "twit twit tooralee ooralee ooralee" of a ruby-crowned kinglet. This was followed by a loud and persistent "freechapel freechapel" from the edge of the spruce, which we hoped would prove to be the Connecticut warbler, for this should be within his range. The mourning warbler, a very similar bird, was common at Mountain Cabin, but so far we had failed to find the Connecticut. After much peering upward through the branchy greenery we located the little songster and were not disappointed, for we could plainly see his identification marks—white eye-ring, and absence of black where grey head met yellow breast.

No mourning warblers were heard or seen here. I have often noticed that where two species resemble each other closely, one will be complimentary in range to the other.

Breakfast over, we donned waders and took to the open, swampy meadow. As we pushed through the willows we heard the cranes, and presently saw a pair standing ostrich-like in the open grass about five hundred yards away. On seeing us they called loudly and commenced to move uneasily. More calls from the farther side of the meadow betrayed the presence of another pair, which we could plainly see with the aid of glasses.

Here in the open it was as nice as the day before, with a cool breeze keeping the insects in check. We commenced a systematic search, separating and walking slowly across the middle of the meadow. It probably contained a thousand acres—partly dry with shortish grass, partly wet with long grass, in places flooded to a depth of four or five inches and supporting a dense growth of dark-green horsetails. Examining these, one could marvel at their construction and easily guess from whence the Indians got the patterns for some of their designs.

The cranes now left the meadow. They moved away from us, calling anxiously. Sometimes they lifted their wide wings and with outstretched necks and legs trailing behind, flew in a short circle; but they always came back, sometimes on one side of us, sometimes on another. We knew they would try to lead us away, and therefore concentrated our search in the vicinity in which we had first seen them, paying particular attention to the wet, reedy border of the lake itself.

It was a lake remarkably like that in the Marais des oiseaux near Jackfish Lake, where some years before I had been successful in finding a breeding colony of Bonaparts gulls. Therefore I was not surprised when—above the cries of godwits, the clattering of rails, and the insistent "peeto" of the hovering black terns—my ears caught an unmistakable harsh scream. Looking up, I found myself being charged by one of these gulls. It proved to be one of several, and although we had no time to locate their nests, they were evidently breeding.

I had found crane's nests before and knew what sort of a bulky structure I ought to find among the tules and cattails. But search as we might, we found neither nest nor young. I stumbled on a sora rail's nest containing eight eggs, and my companion found the nest of a Virginia rail, which he photographed. Red-winged blackbirds had built their deep basket-like nests among the reeds, so conspicuously that they could not escape our attention; and here too, *mirabile dictu,* we found a few pairs of yellow-heads.

Redbreasts and canvasbacks were frequently flushed from their nests, and a pintail with several greenish-yellow ducklings was photographed.

All the time the cranes were in sight, and so uneasy were they that we made sure they were breeding; but we also felt sure that their young were hatched, and a young crane is one of the hardest things in the world to find.

One crane, evidently the male, would call loudly and, stalking along with head held high, allow us to come quite close—close enough to see the bare red forehead plainly—and seem to try to draw us into following him away.

The other bird would stand very quietly and seem to make herself as inconspicuous as possible beside a tuft of grass or reeds. When it seemed that no one was looking, she would bend down in the same attitude as I have seen a turkey hen take when going to her nest, the legs bent to bring the body almost into the grass and the head and neck lower than the back. In this posture she would sneak around behind us. When she kept still we could not see her, which was remarkable considering her size and the fact that her reddish-grey plumage should have been complemented by rather than merged with the surrounding greens.

Many times I pretended to ignore her while covertly watching her movements. She always went in the same direction and hung about very quietly. After giving her plenty of time I would slowly approach, but as soon as I got within about fifty yards she would take wing heavily and, flying low, rejoin her mate.

Although I searched the whole vicinity about which she had been skulking, I could find absolutely nothing and realized that it would take many days to find the young, because each time we desisted from the search the young would probably be moved. Since the sun was now setting and upward of fifteen hours had been spent in vain, we decided to abandon the search and make for camp. My companion had to be in Regina by the end of the week and we had the homeward trip ahead of us, after which he had the fifty-mile journey by canoe to The Pas to catch his train; so this finished our search for this year.

I feel sure the young cranes were there, and given plenty of time I think they could have been found. Cranes are among the wariest of birds and to find them, nests or young, it would seem that one should plan to search a whole area with the greatest thoroughness, regardless of the actions of the birds. All the time we were searching the young birds might have been across the creek in a smaller meadow that we never saw the cranes visit.

I say young birds because, had incubation been in progress, I feel sure that at some time during that fifteen hours the female would have visited the nest lest the eggs get too cold. The young, on the other hand, would be able to obtain food and care for themselves, while the parents amused themselves leading us about.

The homeward journey was much like the trip down, except that we found the current of the Waskwei River against us so strong that we took it in turns to struggle along the rough bank, pulling the canoe with a rope. We camped for the first night at the entrance to Shallow Lake among some lovely willow bushes set in the long blue-joint grass.

On awakening in the morning, the first note we heard was the "cuk cuk cuk" of a cuckoo; and strolling toward the sound I was delighted by the sight of a black-billed one sitting quietly in the midst of a bush. I was so close that I could plainly see the red eye-rim. He uttered his notes once before me and then flew in the quiet, floppy way of his kind to another willow clump, where I left him. This is the farthest north (Township 53) I have ever seen this species.

At the north end of Shallow Lake a phalerope's nest was found and the four pear-shaped eggs photographed as they lay in it.

Recrossing Loon Lake, we found the callas (water arums) now in full bloom, hundreds of them, rearing their waxy white spathes above the dark water. Fain would I have sketched them, but the mosquitoes forbade; so I packed some with moss to take home and draw there.

Embarking again on the Carrot River, we paddled for home. Goldeneyes whistled ahead of us, kingfishers flashed rattling from bank to bank, and once we heard the loud "wheep wheep" of the handsome crested flycatcher from some overhanging birches.

We had hoped to find cranes' nests. Those wary birds had kept their secret; but our search had led to many rich observations.

CHAPTER NINETEEN

Shrouded Trails

THE COLD winter sun is almost down. The trail is drifted deep with
the snow that whips its eternal, restless way over the barren's hum-
mocky surface. Only by feeling with their padded feet for the firmer
trail bottom, built up by the few toboggans which seasonally pass
here, can the huskies avoid floundering.

Soon the faint glow marking the end of the sun's brief visit will
disappear entirely behind the distant spruce ridge, silhouetting it for
a moment and seeming to bring it close. With the light's disappearance one will feel in all its intensity the stark loneliness of the surroundings; but while that glow paints the south-west one still feels
orientated, and seems not far distant from the habitation of one's
kind. Looking into that last reflection, one still sees the world in
the mind's eye as an open map, all places accessible.

There is the south-west, behind that ridge from the top of which
one will come to the headwaters of the familiar Nitenai. To follow
that stream for fifty miles is easy—one cannot get lost. Two blazed
trees—how vividly remembered!—will show us the lobstick portage.
To line up the two lobsticks is a matter of minutes, and then for the
open lake to receive us in friendliness to its smooth, frozen surface.
How the dogs will dash out into this welcome space, and how eagerly
they will make for the little opening visible in the dark line of the
farther shore! Two more days through the snow-burdened woods to
the post, where the almost enveloping night will be pushed back on
both fronts by curtained windows and the mellow glow of oil lamps.
There will be warmth, firelight, laughter, and much talk.

And from the post, as everyone knows, it is but a few days' easy travel down the great river to the railroad town—and from there? Why, from there one can go to Winnipeg! The city! But why stop at Winnipeg when the whole world is within reach? There are the oceans, east and west, the great rolling blue oceans where the breakers roar and hiss; where the spray from their shaggy crests whips one's face, as does the snow in the Keewatin country.

Ah, there is no toilsome plodding up one slope and down the next in this vast liquid barren. Great ships, gold and white and red, with gaily striped funnels and noisy throats, traverse these wastes in calm serenity, their interiors warm and glowing, and savoury with spicy food.

They go to England—merry England, with its breath-taking greenness, its spires, its red-roofed villages. They go to the perfumed Orient, where you can see colour, feel warmth, rub shoulders with white and brown and black and yellow—Arab, Turk, and Parsee, hairy Sikh and plump Bengali, turbanned nomads of the hills, and befezzed ancients of the bazaars.

Life! Human life in all its fullness; richness of sight and sound and smell. The grave murmurings of the elders, the tramp of laden camels at dawn, the shouts of the street vendors; the low, full-throated laughter of the women.

They go to Brazil, Argentina, Chile! Down the grey shores of the east coast, where the fog comes in like a soundless blanket from the Caribbean; across the Gulf, where blue wavelets dance endlessly, their little feet tripping ahead of the happy company whose gay jests ring out from the snowy decks. Along the scented coast to anchor where tinkling guitars strum from white buildings, set amidst a mass of feathery greenness around and behind.

Until the last faint blush fades from the dulling northern sky this map is real and tangible, and the world wherein we move—even this far-off Keewatin—is still tied to it by the questing of the mind's eye, by which we can so safely and so easily follow the trails we know. Faint indeed they are to a stranger, but plain as ribbons of steel to us. So plain that we can take to them almost as instinctively as a dog takes to the homeward road. In our thoughts we can be already miles ahead of the slow-moving dogs. We can feel in anticipation the downward lunge of the toboggan at the river's sudden brink, and note in advance this familiar gnarled tree, that old camping-place.

But the sun has set and there is no moon. The whining wind whips the tiny snow particles into a cold hissing serpent, which writhes across our trail close to the surface of the snow. All distance is lost in a filmy shroud, and the very surface we tread seems to be not of this solid and firm earth. We float, suspended in dreadful silence.

Even the dogs feel the change—the cold pall which surrounds us, the gloom which enfolds us; the sense of drifting, lost and forsaken by all the dear solid things we knew. Above, the northern lights rush like squadrons *en echelon,* their cold silken banners faintly rustling, to do battle with the dark *weetigoes.* They stretch forth their luminous fingers only to withdraw them, ere we have been able to guess their texture. Green and palely gold and faintest rose, they slowly dance the great nightly ballet on a fathomless stage of which the backdrop is eternity, and the wings the edge of the universe.

Still we trudge on step by step, the tightly held toboggan rope the only link with the material world. The dogs move silently, phantom-like, the leaders hardly discernible in the gloom. Only the sharply pointed ears of the nearest show darkly in his own foggy breath-cloud. The toboggan moves as silently as they, seeming not so much to be pulled by them as following them, as a canoe follows the deep, unseen current of the river.

So we all—man and beasts and toboggan—float through the frost fog, straining for the sight of some object. No longer are the dogs spoken to, for the human voice sounds impious in this all-enveloping silence, and the wrath of the lonely places seems very close. The muffled swish of snowshoes, the occasional slaps of the rope, or the rare clink of harness parts, blend themselves with the hissing of the snow to form a murmur which but intensifies the silence, like the rushing sounds in one's ear when one is listening too intently for a call that does not come. It is a murmur which makes us forget everything except that we are drifting on, willy-nilly, scarce aware of the movement of muscles; borne on, rather, by an invisible force which has picked up man, dogs, and load.

With a jar, we stop suddenly. So suddenly that for a moment we are lost and groping; groping for a beautiful peace we cannot remember; groping to touch again that which has lulled us, as a sleeper waking from a happy dream seeks to recall it ere he has to face reality again.

Now action interrupts us. A great fresh snowdrift has formed in a hollow, and the lead dogs are already whining, belly-deep. They are extricated by main force, the trail is found and broken afresh with tramping snowshoes. We seem to have been on the trail for hours. How much further to that timber ridge where we shall camp? All at once we are weary—man and dogs.

But a few moments ago we moved by some great compulsion nor felt that we had aught to do with our drifting progress. Now the dogs lie down with great sighs to regain their wind, licking and worrying their paws to remove the galling ice particles. Sitting on the loaded toboggan, we feel the bite of the sub-zero cold and hunger gnaws. Looking around at the unending, horizonless nothing, we are oppressed by a great and poignant loneliness.

The mind has become too dull now to visualize the map. Winnipeg, England, China—they are but names. They belong to the unattainable. We are here, and there is nowhere else. We are the last living things in the world, and soon we too must be caught up by the wind and dissipated in the fog. With this thought comes a great longing to touch metal, to feel silk, to stand on concrete, to lie and roll and stretch on hard, solid, warm earth; to tread sturdy planking within four walls, where there is form and light and shadow; to be in a crowd and hear a strident band blare down the street; to hear hundreds of voices all around us, so that one may speak—may shout— without fear of the mocking answer of the storm.

Something solid! That's it—something solid to reunite us once more with our mother the earth. Even a tree now. The spruce ridge, the beginning of our almost forgotten map. Got to get to the spruce ridge. Eat. Sleep. We'll take the trail in the morning (will morning ever come?) down the Nitenai, down Lobstick Lake to the post. Sell the dogs—give them away—anything. Hit the trail for the railroad; back to the haunts of man; back to light and laughter and life—"Outside." Away from this gloom, this hell, this tyrant we call the North, where the lights gibber and dance and mock. The North, which slowly, very slowly presses his cold fingers against a man's temples, breathes his cold breath into a man's nostrils, and wraps him in the clammy white shroud which some day will be his last.

And hurry! Hurry! Before it is too late—mush, mush on—the whip cracks hysterically. Will that spruce never show up? Now, just when we have decided to leave it before forgetfulness comes, while we can throw off the spell long enough to see the least bit of our mental-map—has the North played a last trump card against us?

To reach that ridge which was in view before the sun went down, now seems the utmost in attainment.

Oh blessed reality—the spruce trees! Trees dark and straight and sharply pointed as on calender pictures, plain against the now steely sky, for in their shelter the snow wraiths sink to earth and have no more power. We enter their narrow aisles, stretch forth a hand to touch their shaggy bark, and in touching seem again to feel the solid earth in which they are rooted. A white moon slowly rises over the forest of dark spires; and there is the trail, smooth, shiny, and undrifted. The dogs are seen ahead, picked out in light and shadow—friendly Grey and Pishoo, Sport and Rough and Peigan, and patient Boy—good faithful animals once more, not ghosts of the starved North.

They move alertly, pressing their feet on the firm trail; and we are no longer alone, for our shadows are moving alongside like the disembodied things that *we* were, back in that grey haze. The whine of the toboggan and the creak of our good hickory sound friendly and strong and comforting.

Far enough for today, boys. We are within the edge of the map. Camp is soon made, dry wood gathered. And now the ruddy blaze performs its two-fold task—to drive back the cheated shadows and to start the bannock abrowning. The dogs crunch their frozen supper. Hot tea sends up its steaming freshness.

And now, full-fed and safe at last, we can enjoy to the full the great gift of the golden South to the silver North—tobacco—sweet as a ham in a southern oven, fragrant as magnolia.

Well, this is good-bye to the North, we think. Almost regretfully the scene is memorized: the blazing fire lighting up the base of the trees; the good dogs, each curled in his bed; the stout toboggan lying on its side with the firelight playing on the lion's head decorating its curved front—it is a good craft that bears this well-known trademark from Le Pas.

Yes, we must remember scenes like this so that we can describe them to the new friends which we are going to make Outside.

And so to sleep.

A dog rattles a chain; two Canada jays eye the camp for tidbits. Another day has come. In the south-east a red glow grows and grows, and soon the first rays of the sun set afire the tipmost branches of the tallest spruce, putting to shame the glow of last night's fire, now shrunken to grey ashes from which a faint blue wisp still curls upward. We see all the dear familiar things of the forest—the green trees, their lower limbs hung with moss like old men's beards; shoots of red-barked willow sprouting forth from the snow. A squirrel is chattering, the jays are gliding in their silent flight, while a woodpecker—an arctic three-toed—tap-taps his searching way towards the sun.

Our heart leaps with the still beauty of it all—dawn in the wilderness! Clean sweet air, the chuckling notes of the birds. No slaves of the North are we, but free as the lynx padding his hunting trails through the eternal woods. Free to eat and breathe and sleep and travel where we may. Free to go south, to the railroads, to the far Orient or the distant palm shores—free to take the trail or not.

The map is very plain now, but the post is as far as we need to go; for tobacco and tea and flour must be replenished.

Yes, we are as free as the smoke from the moss-chinked cabin to which we shall return ere the break-up wipes away the trails we love so well.

On a night in another winter I snowshoed through a world of sparkling snow. The sky was deep purple-blue, every star like gold. Overhead rode the November moon.

Before me stretched a bush road long forgotten by man, showing only as a break in the skyline of spruce and birch. The small encroaching growth of brush had been so closely browsed by moose that but a few tough twigs pierced the white covering. Across this trail the forms of flanking trees lay etched in deepest shadow.

Only the swish of snowshoes broke the crisp silence. A spruce hen, disturbed by my approach, whirred from its sleep in the snow and disappeared on stiff wings into the shadows.

Around me was the mystery of the moonlit yet shadowy forest. On either hand the evergreens stood straight and patient, content to bear on their limbs the burden of snow which weighed them down.

Behind me the patterns of my snowshoes lay like the links of a chain binding me to the world of music and lamplight. In the unmarked wilderness there is no direction; left or right, forward or back, are all the same. But the faintest trail stumbled upon while roaming the forest instantly recalls one to an orderly world and establishes a definite point from which to survey the surrounding woods; and suddenly, that which but a few moments since was a natural environment appears impenetrable and mysterious.

Here in this silent, windless place, I thought, time seems to be standing still. After all, is not time our most exacting taskmaster, the ruthless robber of our years, whose will is law? For what the hurrying and scurrying of city dwellers but to serve this monster?

In the haunts of men, clocks, railway time-tables, appointment books—a thousand things in a thousand ways—remind us of the saying that time is money. We needs must check it by our timepieces; we must strive to hasten its passing in expectation of some business fulfilment. In the race for money to buy happiness, time—which is money—robs us not only of our youth, our days, our years, but robs us also of the opportunities to attain the greater happiness we cannot buy—a contented mind in tune with nature.

In tune with nature.

Here in the forest all things are rightly ordered, contented, patient. The rotten trees of years gone by, long since fallen before the wind, lie, as they were created to lie, among their living fellows, yielding to them the richness of their woods.

The living trees—beautiful trees, thousands of them never to be seen by men—stand each in its appointed place, each fulfilling the purpose for which it sprung up; waiting patiently for spring to be followed by summer and summer by another winter.

How few of us fulfil our destiny as do these trees and the wild things of the prairies and woods!

So I thought, as I stood silently on my snowshoes in the crisp night.

I turned homeward; and the forest stood just as it had stood before I went for my walk, and would stand always; but I had received its message.

The whip of the blizzard, the creak of saddle-leather, the grating of a canoe keel, all strike a chord and bear a message. It may be a grey message of death in the wilderness. It may be a message to conquer and attain. It may be a message of love, waking the heart as a pony's hooves waken the grass birds.

But the message of the silent places is the key to a proper understanding of all the others. Listening to it, we realize that only in our own minds are things not right, well ordered, and as they should be; and if we can but absorb the atmosphere of orderliness and patience with which we are surrounded, we shall come to find that in the Creator's scheme, as nowhere else, stand the two words—Faith and Hope.

This was good-bye to the woods—but I knew I should see them again.

The war drums were throbbing again across the water; even here in the wilderness their echoes penetrated.

The campfire was cold.

The trail was before me.

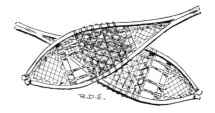